HOME-BASED TREATMENT

Pirkko Karvonen

HOME-BASED TREATMENT

in the life stories
of Finnish young people

Translation is based on the original in Finnish: *Rajojen rikkojat - kotikuntoutus nuorten elämäntarinoissa* (Karvonen, 2015)

Cover picture by Tiia Keskiaho

Publisher: Books on Demand GmbH, Helsinki, Suomi;
Manufacturer: Books on Demand GmbH, Norderstedt, Saksa.
ISBN: 978-952-330-384-3

A little girl was severely disabled. She refused to go out and play so that nobody would see her.

- I can't stand people staring at me, she said to her parents.

- Those people who stare have been infected with a staring sickness, her mother told.

- Only people like you can cure them.

- How come? asked the girl

- Look them in the eye and say: I am doing fine - how about you?

- When you see them turning red, you know that they have been cured from the staring sickness, with your help.

It is amazing how many persons the little girl has been able to cure.

(Positiivari-magazine, 1996)

CONTENTS

To the reader

This book describes the life stories of young adults who have participated in the Kerland/Brainwave home-based treatment program. Rehabilitation conducted at home requires strength, patience and money from the family. Without external assistants this kind of rehabilitation would not be possible.

The life stories were collected from accounts of nearly 30 years´ time. Most of these young adults were born premature. The moment of birth was extremely critical and *the thread of life was very thin*, as one mother said. Almost all of these young adults have cerebral palsy and some of them also other disturbances in development. The life stories describe the lives of these young adults during the years.

The Finnish health care experts didn't give much future prospects for the children, so their parents had a strong feeling that hope for their child's development was taken from them in Finland. The knowledge of different, foreign rehabilitation methods, where the parents were active in their child's rehabilitation, tempted the parents to give them a try.

This book tells about the Kerland Centre, which came into the awareness of Finnish families at the beginning of the 1990's, and the families participating in the program. The Kerland Centre answered the parents' need to participate in their child's rehabilitation in larger amount than it was possible in Finland at that time. The name of the Centre changed into Brainwave Centre with the new owners. In this book I use the name Kerland/Brainwave due to the fact that most of the Finnish families participated in the program already before the name was changed. First the families traveled to England but later on the Centre opened a receptioncentre in Kankaanpää, Finland also.

The Finnish health care experts criticized the foreign rehabilitation method, sometimes with quite strong wordings. They saw that the theory base of the rehabilitation didn't base enough on scientific research and that the parents cannot act as the rehabilitator of their own child. Despite all this, the parents had the courage to question the traditional Finnish concepts of parents' participation in supporting their own child's development.

The life stories of the children are based on the memories of the children and of their parents, but the most important parts are the current affairs. Some of the young adults were able to write themselves and I edited those texts to fit into this book. Other life stories are based on what the parents have told. Also some young adults have their siblings describing their memories.

I started the interviews in the summer of 2013 and added some information during the following years. The interviews took place in the homes of the families all around Finland. The families were selected on the basis of them I was able to reach after such a long time since the start of the rehabilitation.

The life stories start with description of childhood and problems with birth. Then, how home-based treatment was realized and its benefits are described. The book also describes school years of the children and their life today, what are they doing now, where they live and what kind of choices they have made in life.

The functioning principles of the Kerland/Brainwave Centre are described in this book and also the background history and how the Centre was brought to Finland. Some of the young adults tell the story of their travel to England with their parents.

The idea to write this book has been influenced by my possibility to follow the life of one of the young adults in this book, Juha, and his rehabilitation by the home-based treatment program from the first years onwards. I visited the Kerland/Brainwave Centre with Juha's family a couple of times and I wrote a book of Juha's rehabilitation years called *Juhan askeleet* (Karvonen, 1999). Many years afterwards I had the pleasure of attending Juha's wedding. And there I had the idea of finding out how the other young adults are doing, who participated in the home-based treatment program at the same time as Juha. Has life offered them times of happiness or difficulty? Looking back, has the home-based treatment been of any use? What kind of plans for the future they have? Inspired by these questions I decided to start collecting the life stories of these young adults.

The young adults and their families in this book have been breaking the limits and surpassing them in many ways. These young adults have been lucky enough to have such parents who had the courage and strength to fulfill sometimes heavy home-based treatment during several years. Here are the stories of Juha, Jutta, Louhi, Memme, Salla, Sanni, Tiia, Unsku and Veikko told together with their families. All the poems in the book are by one of the young adults, Jutta, from her book *Keneen lie tullut* (Selänpää, 2009).

Jyväskylä, February 15th, 2016
Pirkko Karvonen

Journey of my life

*I remember my childhood
when I was planning my future.
I was dreaming about everything; I didn't know what real life is.
I thought life never changes.
One day my journey started. It was more difficult than I thought.
My parents taught me how to move on.*

*Every year I grew up, my journey proceeded.
There were sometimes turns-off, I lost my childhood.
A year after one, I came back to the old school.
We shared happy moments with classmates,
we let bad days go away.
I had my first love.
My family supported me at home.*

*Now I have lived my life.
So many kilometers.
My journey moves on.
I think I never want it to stop.
I can still live my life with you.
Someday the destination will wait for me,
stop my journey.
I'm moving on the unknown way.
Through the troubles.
I will live my life with you.*

The basis for holistic rehabilitation

The Finnish families of disabled children found out about foreign rehabilitation Centres via magazines and books published abroad. In the United States they developed rehabilitation methods for disabled adults already in the 1950's. Glenn Doman, who had been educated as a physiotherapist, had the idea of the rehabilitation when he was treating adults who had been injured to the head in the World War II.

Rehabilitation for children was developed later on. The main work in his career Doman has done in developing rehabilitation for children with brain injuries. He has received help in this work from a team that was composed of experts in child development, doctors, teachers, brain surgeons and psychologists. The main characters, in addition to Doman, in this development work have been Carl Delacato and Temple Fay.

In addition to rehabilitation for disabled children, the working group also studied the brain development of healthy children. During the years, the paths of these main characters have gone their own ways probably due to differences in point of view.

In 1955 Doman established an institution and he has acted as the director of it for the rest of his life. The Institute for the Achievement of Human Potential is located in Philadelphia, in The United States. The institute has side offices in different parts of the world, like in Japan, Italy, Spain, Mexico, Australia and Norway.

The rehabilitation program for brain injured children is based on neurological development which consists of three sensoric (vision, auditory and tactile) and of three motoric parts (mobility, language and manual). In the rehabilitation, the development of the usage capacity of the brain and wide usage of brain through many sensoric channels are worked on at the earliest possible phase. New bridges are built via sensoric stimulus to pass the injured parts in the brain. With frequent repetition the feeling, hearing and eyesight are stimulated and thus the new brain areas are made to perform tasks that the injured areas cannot perform. In the background there is a strong view of plasticity of the brain.

In addition to the rehabilitation of disabled children, The Doman Institute also arranges courses to the parents of healthy children of how they can advance the use of the brain capacity of their children and thus learning. Doman has published several books and some of them are listed in the references of this book.

Doman also visited Finland in 1985 through an invitation of a few active mothers. He gave a five-day course to a small group that mostly consisted of the parents of disabled children. *New points of view for the rehabilitation of children, who require special care and upbringing and for supporting the early development of healthy children* was the title of the seminar. During the visit to Finland, Doman expressed his interest in establishing his Institute in Finland, but the official health care system in Finland wasn't ready for it.

After the 5-day course Doman gave brief and general consultation to the families who asked for it. For example, he gave advice to the mother of a five year-old, dysphasic boy as follows: 1. Leave out junk food. No sweets, no additives. Food as organic as possible. 2. Practice handling of a ball with your child in different ways, like throwing, rolling and catching. This advances finding the chirality and strengthens eye-hand coordination. 3. Persuade your child to move, that is how his oxygen intake increases. Swimming and especially diving and also running and skiing are preferred sports. In those the child will practice reciprocity of his limbs. 4. Play with the reading cards with your child. There are whole, single words written on the cards that are shown to the child. The words are written with bigger font and they are connected to the interest of each child.

Six months after Doman's visit, a couple of us who organized his seminar in Finland had the opportunity to travel to Philadelphia to a course called *What To Do About Your Brain-Injured Child* and get better acquainted with the Institute. There were people from all around the world attending the week-long course. We were given lectures and demonstrations. Doman himself was the main lecturer who told us about the different phases of the Institute and its functioning principles.

After about five years since Doman`s visit to a broader discussion was started about the possibility to get rehabilitation from abroad that would engage active parents in doing more themselves for the development of their child. This hope started to materialize when families received information about the Centres in England and Belgium.

Kerland/Brainwave centre and its functioning principles

The English Kerland Centre was established when one of the founding members had studied in the Doman Institute in Philadelphia. After returning to England he founded the Kerland Centre in 1982. The name of the Centre was changed to Brainwave Centre in 1995 when the leaders of the Centre were changed. (www.brainwave.org.uk)

The current director of the Brainwave Centre, Phil Edge, says that at the moment the Centre is functioning only in England. Many years ago Brainwave Centre was active also in Switzerland, Japan and Finland. But in England the necessity of services was growing steadily and so finally the activities were centralized in England and ended in other countries.

Brainwave Centre was established in Finland in 1993 and during the next 10 years the therapists of the Centre consulted in Finland. However, all the families first traveled to England for the first evaluation. The Brainwave Centre evaluates that there have been over 50 children with their families participating in the program. Another Nordic country visiting the Centre was Sweden. There were only a couple of Swedish families and Kerland/Brainwave didn't open a branch in Sweden.

The aim of the Brainwave Centre is to help children with disabilities and additional needs to achieve better independence. The activities also aim to add mobility, communication skills and learning potential of these children through multiple learning and physical therapies.

The programs designed for the children are meant to be done with the help of the family. The programs are planned based on two-day evaluation in one of the therapy Centres in England (Somerset, Essec, Chesire).

The first day is spent by the therapy team evaluating the abilities of the child and they also discuss with the parents of their goals and hopes. Sometimes the child is also present at these discussions. This requires a lot of work because the described exercises must be achievable. When the therapists have designed the program, the second day is spent teaching the exercises to the parents so that they are able to execute them at home.

The parents are given all the needed equipment and materials to execute the program. Nowadays there are supporting therapists and family assistants who keep regular contact with the families. At the moment Brainwave Centre employs physiotherapists, occupational therapists, speech therapists and educational therapists who work together in order to offer a rehabilitation program for the child. Each 4 – 6 months the families return to one of the centers for follow-up evaluation where the progress of the child is monitored and the program is changed to reflect the progress. The basic aim for each child is to achieve the greatest possible independence at their developmental level.

There are children at the Brainwave Centre who have multiple diagnosis and injuries. The ages of the children vary from six months to 12 years; however most of them are under five years old. The analysis made at the end of 2014 showed that the most common diagnosis were as follows:

Cerebral Palsy   33%
Developmental delay   20%
Down syndrome   7%
Autism   8%
Chromosome anomaly   8%
Unknown diagnosis   3%
There were also other diagnoses (21%) such as meningitis,
rare genetic disorders or disorders as a consequence of an accident.

The Brainwave Centre celebrated its 30th jubilee in 2012. During that time, over 2000 children have received evaluation at the center. According to Phil Edge, there hasn't been any quantitative research due to it being too expensive, but the universities of Bournemouth and West-England have conducted two qualitative researches. In both of them Brainwave was seen in a very positive light. These researches were made by interviewing many of the families who participated in the Brainwave program and the majority of them (over 80%) showed that the program had had a positive impact on their child.

A collection of the development of the children was made in 2014. There were 599 children who participated in this and who had achieved developmental goals that they had not been able to achieve before. This has a direct impact on the everyday life of the children themselves and for their families and they can be perceived as life-altering achievements. The most common developmental steps were walking independently, crawling and creeping, using fork and knife, using toilet independently, sitting down independently, learning to roll over and taking eye contact for the first time.

Brainwave has been active for over 30 years and thus it is clear that the therapy programs have changed over the years. The latest addition is the Sensory integration. Another big developmental step is the use of technology. Laptops and iPads have established themselves as standard equipment in some of the programs and they help children to learn, to focus and to communicate. In addition, development in the efficiency of physical techniques and equipment, have made it possible for the children to become more independent as movers than it has been possible before.

Kerland/Brainwave Centre in Finland

When the families heard of a possibility to go to England to the Kerland Centre to receive an evaluation of their child and a home-based treatment program for home, many of them were very enthusiastic. At first the families had to travel to England with their disabled child a couple of times a year, which might have been problematic. So a thought came up to establish the Centre in Finland.

However, it took some time before the Centre was established in Finland. Pirkko Karvonen and documentary director Tarja Tallqvist visited the Kerland Centre in 1991 and after that the active planning to get the Centre in Finland was started. Several contacts and exchange of messages was required with the directors of the center at that time. We invited them to come to Finland for the negotiations, because they had negotiations going on at the same time with Sweden and Norway. The directors back then, Margaret Baker and Trevor England, came to Helsinki, Finland on January 20th 1992. We organized a meeting with the ministry of social and health affairs. The goal of that meeting was to get the official Finland also to take part in this. The result was, however, that the officials of social and health ministry didn't get convinced. Establishing a foreign rehabilitation centre to Finland was a strange idea to them.

After the visit the parents started to organize everything in order to get the Kerland Centre to Finland. The families decided to establish an association to promote the matter. The association for the home-based treatment of brain-injured children, RAMPPI, was established in 1992 and Professor Pekka Mäenpää was elected chairman. In the beginning there were about 20 families. The association communicated with the families and the Kerland/Brainwave Centre regularly with newsletters and organized a yearly meeting where foreign and domestic experts were invited as speakers. Many towns were considered as the location of the Centre and finally the city of Kankaanpää was selected thanks to the activity of one father's active input. The Brainwave Centre started its activities in Finland in 1993 and the new director of the Centre, Phil Edge, agreed to visit Finland once or twice a year.

The RAMPPI association was active during 10 years' time but new families didn't take part and the rehabilitation of the children of member families was already directed elsewhere. The activities of the Kerland/Brainwave Centre were ceased at that time.

The families in this book have all taken part in the Kerland/Brainwave Centre's program. Some of the families also took part in the Delacato Centre's program at the same time. In addition, all the families received traditional Finnish rehabilitation which meant physiotherapy or other kind of therapy approximately twice a week.

The press got interested in Kerland/Brainwave Centre coming to Finland. Many families got to tell about their experiences for magazines and TV.

Human

I want to be here, not elsewhere.
I want to be slow, not fast.
I want to do good, not to do harm.
I want to be just myself, not anyone else.
I want to be silent, not loud.
I want to heal, not to hurt.
I want to grow, not to break.
I want to write, not just to read.
I want to remember good moments, not bad ones.
I want to paint, not to mess.
I want to be normal, not a monster.
I want to listen to You, not anyone else.
I want to be Your friend, nothing else.

Life stories of the young

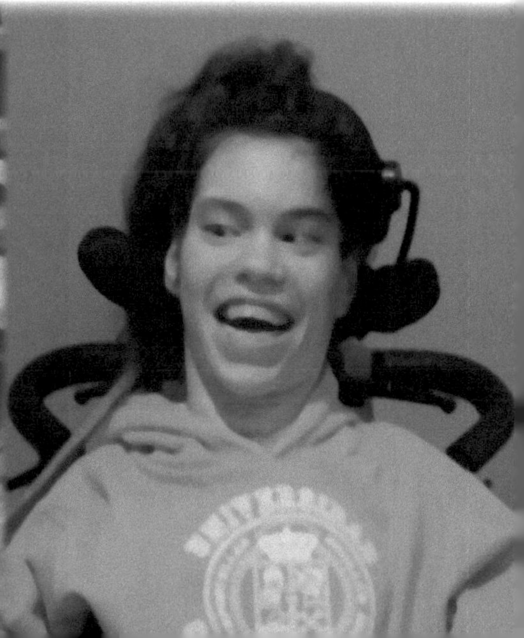

Juha

CHILDHOOD

Juha is the first-born of the family. He was born premature, two and a half months too early. At the age of six Juha stated: *I was born extremely small, brain-injured*. The head of this boy, the size of a milk carton, was bruised and he had heart murmurs. His lifetime was estimated by the hour. For the first four weeks he spent in the incubator.

Age: 28 years

Home-based treatment started at the age of four

Home-based treatment lasted three years

Learned to walk at the age of six

IT expert

Juha's mother was scared to sleep thinking that her child might die during that time. Death was lurking over the shoulder all the time and the mother just prayed for her child's survival. When Juha was sent home he suffered from baby colic and could cry 16 hours a day. His development was slow, but the mother received soothing words like: *Premature babies just develop more slowly; you don't have to worry about it.*

Juha was very spastic. At the age of one he received the diagnosis of cerebral palsy (diplegia spastica) and his possibilities to walk, talk or function couldn't be predicted. He was offered a wheelchair for permanent use at the age of three, but her parents refused that because then Juha would get accustomed to it and wouldn't even try to walk. Juha could stand up only when supported. While creeping his fingers were clenched and when crawling he moved forward with scooping movement with his hands while his legs followed passively. His breathing was disturbed with abruptions as if it would run out.

When Juha was one year old he was given Finnish physiotherapy twice a week. In addition the parents were taught to handle and lift him correctly. But this wasn't enough for the parents; they were willing to do much more for their child.

HOME-BASED TREATMENT

Juha was nearly four years old when the Kerland program was started in 1991. The program was executed during three years' time. The parents did appreciate the Finnish rehabilitation, but they thought it wasn't enough. Juha's development wouldn't have progressed with only two hours of physiotherapy in a week. The Kerland program was executed three hours a day, 15 hours a week.

When Juha's family heard about the English Kerland Centre where parents were taught to rehabilitate their child at home, they immediately decided to find more about it. The decision to go to the Kerland Centre was fast and after six months they already were in England. From there started a regular, daily home-based treatment which lasted for a couple of years.

The home-based treatment was the mother's responsibility because the father had to work to get money for everything. The mother had several assistants helping her in the rehabilitation. When the treatment started the home had to be open for all the different people. But for the mother this was her lifeline to the outside world.

For Juha meeting a new assistant was a good chance to discuss his favorite topic of cars and especially what defects the cars of the assistants had. Juha was an eager Lada fan at that time. The assistants had the patience to discuss, tell stories and sing with Juha.

All the assistants didn't want to continue after their first time because they thought that the rehabilitation exercises were torture to the child. Once when a new assistant, who didn't know anything about this rehabilitation method, came to the house and saw Juha hanging from his ankles from the ceiling, he turned away. Juha's ankles were tied to a rope and the rope was safely hanging from the ceiling hooks. On top of everything Juha was screaming while hanging, but he was screaming of joy.

How the day of home-based treatment proceeded

The daily treatment program was divided into six parts and each of them lasted for half an hour so there were in all three hours of treatment a day. In the morning from eight until eleven four parts were done. Then there was a lunch break and Juha went to play either outside or inside with his assistant. During that time the mother had a moment to handle other things, bake, clean or even to rest. The program continued in the afternoon at two when two parts of it were done. The rest of the evening was free time and then the family visited friends or did other things belonging to a daily life. Also weekends were free and then the family liked to go to their summer cottage during summer time. If some part of the program wasn't done during the day, it was done in the evening with father.

During three years' time Juha had a total of five different home-based treatment programs. Below is the first of them which contained balance, breathing, modeling and standing exercises and watching word cards.

1. Breathing exercise: Mask (5x1min)
2. Word cards
3. Hip Unlocking (4x1min)
4. Trunkal Pattern (1x3min)
5. Cross Pattern (2x3min)
6. Horizontal ladder:"walking" along by moving hands
7. Head-down hanging from the ceiling (3x1min)
8. Standing against a support
9. "Hot potato" balancing exercise

Juha woke up normally around 6 a.m. when his father started making coffee. At eight a.m. the doorbell rang and Juha's personal assistant came to help with the exercises. After a while came Juha's grandmother and then the daily program could be started.

During the exercises there was usually background music, it was something cheery or children's songs. At the same time Juha's favorite toy, Freddie the Frog jumped on the modeling table. Freddie usually sat beside Juha and he helped in many tasks. Juha's mother told brave adventures of Freddie the Frog and his friends at the frog pool. Freddie also discussed with Juha with the help of one of the assistants. *Juha, where is your police office nowadays,* asked Freddie. While Juha is listening to Freddie's questions he is breathing through a mask for one minute's time, which helps him to breathe more strongly than normal.

An alarm sounds off when it's time to end the exercise with the mask. Juha answers all the questions from Freddie and presents him with additional questions. Juha's imagination is set free when the assistant calls to the Chief of Police and tells that there is a dangerous thief on the loose. At the same time body patterning is done to Juha with the help of two assistants and the third assistant is telling more and more wild stories of the thief getting caught according to the instructions of the Chief of Police. The phone call ends just when the alarm goes off again.

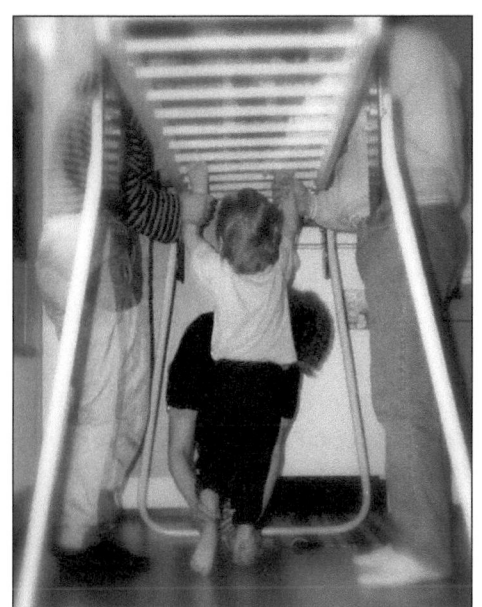

Horizontal ladder.

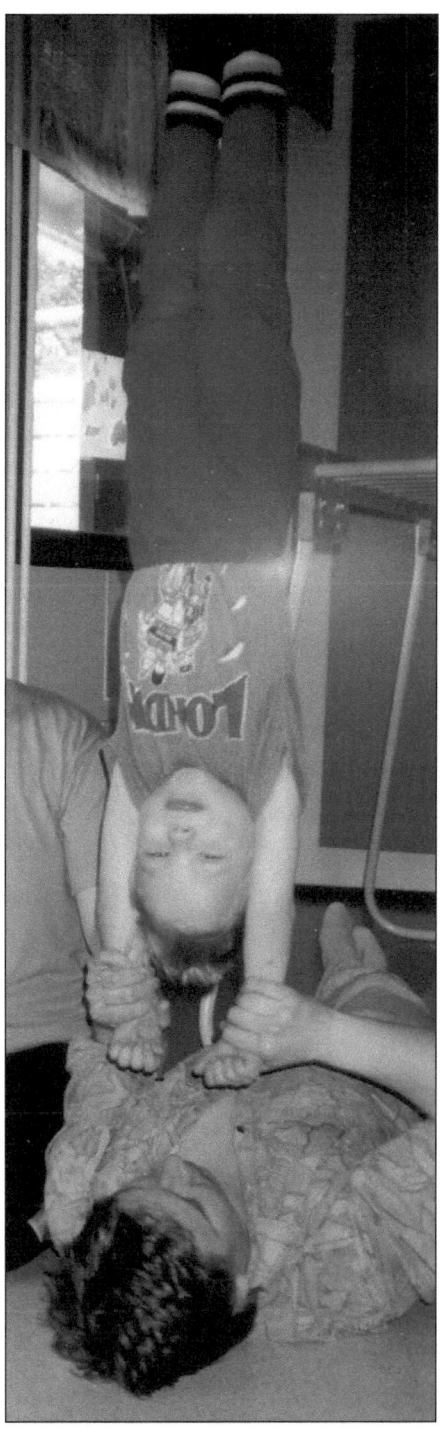

Head-down hanging from the ceiling and stretching

Next, Freddie the Frog asks for a bumpy ride because he thinks it is most fun. Bumpy ride is done by walking along the horizontal ladders. It is done so that two assistants move Juha's hands above his head in turns from one step to the next. At the same time one assistant moves Juha's feet forward from his ankles in turns. This is how taking steps correctly is modeled. There is a thick boom on the floor which is meant to keep the feet separate. Juha is also asked to step very strongly with his feet and this is how the bumpy ride is produced. An alarm gives indication to move to the next exercise.

In the middle of Hip Unlocking Juha recalls suddenly that grandmother's Lada-car hasn't been working correctly lately. *Grandma, don't you go and sell your car. You have to save it until I turn eighteen. I will buy it from you then and put a roof hatch and a golden gearstick,* Juha promises. *I wonder if you will have it anymore then*, grandmother asks. Again, the alarm gives indication that it is time to move to the next exercise, but Juha's questions regarding the interesting topic continue. In cross patterning three assistants are needed: one is turning Juha's head, second is moving Juha's left arm and leg and the third is moving his right-side limbs. This is the longest exercise during which Juha and his grandmother continue their conversation about the Lada. Juha gives his grandmother good advice for fixing the Lada.

There is still the mask exercise left from the half an hour part of the program, and also watching the word cards, walking on a ramp and the balancing and motion sensory exercises (vestibular exercises), which are meant to give Juha the sensation of his body's different postures and movements. Straps are put around Juha's ankles and they are fastened to a rope hanging from the ceiling. Juha is hanging head-down and swinging from side to side or he is set into a spinning motion. *Don't you tickle me, grandma! The world seems very different looking from upside-down*, Juha chatters. The conversation is continuous without a pause almost the entire half an hour time. Only the alarm gives a little break for the conversation and the exercises.

In the afternoon at half-past one it is time for coffee and plans for the next weekend are made. After that it is time for the last parts of the daily program. The assistant was a student of health and social services who came to assist with the rehabilitation program regularly, once a week. *What's up, Juha?* asks the student and immediately starts Juha's long story of the week-end trip to ice-fishing with his uncle. At the same time leg muscle strengthening exercises are done to Juha, which means standing up exercises. The assistant asks Juha to stretch his legs more strongly because doing the actual exercise sometimes is forgotten in the midst of a lively conversation. When Juha is doing very well in some exercise, he is praised by all of the assistants.

Juha had also physio- and occupational therapy some evenings during the week and he went to a music club with his father. Juha usually went to sleep around nine p.m. and the next morning the same daily program exercises continued, but with new stories and usually with new assistants.

Home-based treatment and its benefits

During the tight home-based treatment program clear changes started to appear. First signs of progress were that Juha's breathing got better and thus his speech became clearer and he started sleeping the whole night through. Earlier Juha woke up several times a night. The importance of the rehabilitation was especially shown on his physical strength and bodily functions getting better.

At first the new program seemed a bit hard for Juha but he got used to it gradually. Freddie the Frog was very important to Juha when he was younger. Freddie helped him to cope when he felt he didn't have the strength to go on. Juha still wonders how his mother could invent every time new stories of Freddie and what he had done. Juha disliked patterning the most. Hanging head-down from his feet was his favorite exercise.

At the age of six Juha learned to walk short distances. He was very happy about it and said: *For me, it feels wonderful to be happy because I have learned to walk and to cycle, read and write. But one thing I miss, and that is being able to run. It was worth doing the home-based treatment. I'm glad I didn't give up. Now it has been accomplished.* Learning to walk was a big surprise for health care professionals and also to Juha's parents, because they were told a few years back that this child would never become a walking person.

The tight treatment made Juha's muscles stronger which helped him to get accepted to rhizotomy operation. Rhizotomy is neurosurgery where spinal nerves are cut in order to lessen spasticity, which means abnormally strong muscle tension and which hinders movement. Precondition for the surgery was that the child was in good physical form, was willing to have the surgery and to the demanding cooperation years ahead. The physiotherapist was amazed at Juha's muscles and how good shape they were in. He said that he had never seen a child with so noticeable muscles. Also the doctor had said that to this boy The Kerland/Brainwave treatment has laid a foundation for the so-called traditional physiotherapy that continued from there.

This is how Juha has developed constantly regarding his physical condition. Juha himself thinks that the home based treatment had a central role in the development of his physical condition during the time the program was practised. He says that it is probable that no other choice would have given the same results in that situation. He feels lucky having received so much rehabilitation in different forms, both Kerland/Brainwave and traditional Finnish rehabilitation.

Juha´s treatment is described in a book about this time called Juha's steps (Juhan askeleet, Karvonen 1999). Juha also wrote one chapter to it himself where he describes the home-based treatment from a 12 year-old's point of view: "The home-based treatment has given me the benefits of learning to walk pretty well and moving around independently. Inside I can move short distances without walking sticks and the rest I walk with them. Outside I use walking frame. I remember the visits to England as very positive and supportive. Maybe because I received such positive feedback from there. I remember some of the staff at Kerland Centre, for example James. I liked the way he whistled. The only thing I disliked about going to the Centre was that we had to leave dad home. Now that I'm older I understand that we didn't have limitless amount of money to spend.

I think Kerland/Brainwave program is a good one, but hard. The most important thing before starting this program is to consider carefully if your physical and mental resources are enough and if you are ready to give up some of your free time. I can tell you that the end result is good and rewarding. To all who consider starting home-based treatment program I want to say: You can do it!"

Juha is grateful to his own parents because they have worked hard even though they were criticized at times with harsh words. He is also grateful to all his assistants. With all this help Juha has reached a situation where he can live independently with some assistance.

Juha's parents felt that it would be important to tell about this home-based treatment to others interested in it. So they presented it to, for example, health care students a couple of times. This way they also got assistants to help out with the treatment exercises. When Juha was at junior high school he gave presentations with a blind student regarding disability and home-based treatment to other students. This was to help raise awareness and change attitudes and as Juha recalls the auditorium was miraculously silent and impressed after their presentation.

Experiences with the Finnish health care staff

When the family started the home-based treatment program they were observed very carefully. At first the mother felt herself insecure when talking with the health care staff regarding starting the home-based treatment program, but gradually her own thoughts and reasoning for it grew stronger. *At first I was always asking forgiveness for my existence. All that was said to us, we believed. During the years we learned that the doctors are not superhuman. We have become bolder and aren't afraid of making our own choices.*

One unpleasant memory is still alive from those years. During the time Juha was in hospital he was put under a scrutiny of the health care staff. This happened when the family had visited England the first time and received a new rehabilitation program. The mother was stopping by at the hospital cafeteria and during that time Juha had been placed on a table. Suddenly the room had been full of people who started to ask him all sorts of things. *Do you have the strength to do that home-based treatment at home? Are you hurting? Do you even want to do it? Are you afraid?* When this situation was informed to the mother she got so angry and criticized the behavior of the health care staff: *You can ask questions from Juha only in the presence of us, his parents.*

Despite these negative experiences there were also some persons in the health care staff that believed, supported and saw the possibilities of home-based treatment for the child.

The long experience working with the hospital staff during childhood gave Juha a clear insight on what a good assistant is like: *A good assistant is the kind who loosens up when you tell her to loosen up.* From doctors Juha has both good and bad experiences: *That doctor had lost his reputation. He didn't think before opening his mouth. He said to me that my walking isn't pretty and I should stay in the wheelchair. That neurologist really pushed my buttons. I thought in my mind that don't you dare try and say something like that or I'll....* Juha respected those doctors who treated him in a humane manner: *When that nice doctor comes across in the hall he doesn't just say hello, but hello Juha and pats my head. He remembers each child by the looks every time.*

MEMORIES FROM SCHOOL YEARS

The first school years went quite well, according to Juha. He sometimes had moments of fear because there was a boy in his class who used to bully all the children. Juha told his mother of these experiences and threatened to punch the bullies if he just could. His mother gave advice to Juha: *Let your words talk when you cannot use strength.* When some of Juha's classmates called him brain injured, Juha gave them advice to go to the library and find out what is written of the matter. And then they could come and discuss with him.

During the first years at school Juha felt sad about not being able to participate in playing games that required running. However sometimes Juha forgot about the limits of his movement. Once, when the teacher asked who wanted to participate in long jump and running competition at a sports day at school, Juha also raised his hand with the others.

Then one of his classmates noted that Juha cannot participate and the whole class fell silent. Juha still insisted why he couldn't participate and his classmates said: *Because you cannot run.* After a moment's thought Juha realized the situation himself and started laughing.

In addition, playing football or ice-hockey wasn't possible. The boys however chose Juha as their coach and Juha gave instructions on how to score a goal and he shouted instructions during the game also. When the team scored a goal they all patted Juha's head as a thank you.

During the first years of school Juha experienced his first crisis of being disabled. He pondered a lot of being different and tried to find acceptance of his disability in himself.

There were times when Juha didn't even want to go out to play with other children: *What would I do outside, there is nothing to do. I am slow and I cannot catch the other children but they catch me very easily. They don't want to play cops and thieves with me. I cannot climb a tree, others pass me while running and I am always the last one.*

After elementary school Juha went to high school which lasted for him five years. He passed almost all the compulsory courses and graduated from four subjects, except for mathematics. Juha admits not putting enough effort on studying at high school. He was more interested in partying with friends, girls and other activities typical of that age.

LIFE TODAY

Juha is a 28-year-old young man who is quite resilient and determined, according to him. The Kerland/Brainwave home-based treatment has had a great impact on his quality of life and he is very grateful for that.

At the moment Juha is living in northern Finland, about 400 kilometres from his childhood home. He moved to northern Finland with his new girlfriend back then, but the eight-year relationship ended up in divorce in 2014. He was devastated for some time, but luckily he has close friends and family who have helped and supported him. For all of them Juha wants to give recognition.

Now, more than a year after the divorce, Juha's life is back on track again. He has met a wonderful new woman and they are living together at the moment. The future looks bright.

Juha tells he leads similar everyday life as any adult, but with a difference that he has problems with his ability to function. He manages it well, but still needs some assistance. His personal assistant helps him with hobbies and with some household chores he would do himself if he could. This way he can also contribute to the relationship as an equal partner. This is very important to Juha, because he doesn't want to burden his girlfriend excessively due to his disability so that she wouldn't feel herself as his assistant but his girlfriend.

At home Juha walks mainly without aiding equipment, only leaning on to furniture at times. His principal aid with walking is the walking frame. When needed, he also uses a wheelchair when he has to travel several kilometers or when he is temporarily unable to walk due to sickness or injury.

Juha has many hobbies and he likes to spend time with his friends, go to movies and to sport events. He is active on Twitter and Instagram. Sometimes Juha goes out to dinner with his friends or to bars and at times they hold game nights with console games in a bigger crowd.

Physical exercise is very important to Juha in many forms. He receives guided physiotherapy and in addition he takes care of his own physical health in free time. His most passionate hobby is exercising his muscle strength both at home and in the gym. His latest hobby is martial arts for self- defense purposes.

Juha thinks that the amount of treatment is directly comparable to the ability to function, to move and to an independent life. He thinks that disabled people require much more treatment than they get. He has also learned that one must put effort into voluntary physical exercise every day. One cannot give up, there is no other option. If there is a four weeks' break in the rehabilitation/exercise, you notice it immediately in your body, says Juha. In order to get into shape that you were in before the break, you must work double the amount. Juha sees that if you want to exercise your ability to function on the maximum level (especially when you are disabled), it takes a very disciplined, goal-oriented and professional athlete –like way of life.

Computers have always been part of Juha's life since he was six years old. All recreational electronics, movies, music, literature and following sports interest him in many forms. Especially crime fiction is his favorite read. This might come from his childhood dream of becoming a police officer. In addition, the daily politics have importance to him and Juha isn't afraid of taking a stance on social injustices. He follows politics from many different sources.

Facts of life

Juha sees that his disability has made his life harder in many ways and some things have been impossible to him, but still he wouldn't change a day. Through his disability he has been able to experience things he wouldn't have without his disability. In addition, he has met so many people he wouldn't have met ever, most likely. The best example of this is Juha's friend Vesa, who is the son of Juha's first physiotherapist. Juha says that they have had a deep connection since childhood already. Even though being disabled brings difficulties and limitations to some parts in life, Juha says he lives a full life just like any other young adult. There are rocky parts as there are peaks in life, just like everybody.

Juha doesn't need any special treatment, but he requires financial equality compared to other people. Disabled don't have same chances of employment as healthy people, due to their disability. Juha wishes for a better basic security than society can offer today. Juha thinks that people born disabled are doomed to poverty because most of them cannot get employed realistically. None of them can buy their own house with just the guaranteed pension. The pension, which disabled people receive, is not even close to the monthly pay of a basic worker. Those people who have been disabled due to an accident or some brain injury during their life mostly receive a work pension and the luckiest ones have a life insurance. People born disabled don't receive these benefits.

Depressing attempts to get a job

Juha has tried to apply for a job but with no success. He has experienced many misfortunes, like other disabled must have. Juha sees that he has been rejected many times by the employers solely because he is disabled. He has noticed that from the facial expressions, body language and the general attitude of the interviewer.

"I went to the unemployment agency to talk about my situation. Together we decided with the official there to try and find me a job. It was about a supported employment which means that I would be basically free workforce to the company. One local IT company in the nearby city seemed interested when the unemployment agency called them and asked about the possibility and willingness to this kind of arrangement.

The company was interested so they asked me to tell more about myself and what skills I had via e-mail. I made a CV for them where I compiled all necessary information and sent the e-mail. Pretty quickly I received an answer telling me that they were very interested.

The note said that: *There is always a job for a guy like you.* I thought that this was great, for once something seemed to get organized because their interest towards me seemed real. We made arrangements for a job interview and everything seemed to go smoothly. I collected all my school and work certificates for the interview. I had been working short, couple of weeks of work practices in an IT company in my town and for the city's IT support. Both of them gave me good reference and work certificates and they were very pleased with my skills and the quality of my work.

The day of the interview came and I went there in good time and with all my papers. The secretary received me and inquired whom I wanted to see. I told that I had an appointment with the CEO for a job interview. The secretary confirmed the fact from her computer and went to tell the CEO of my arrival. The secretary came back shortly and said that the CEO would receive me in a couple of minutes.

The CEO came to me, shook my hand and we changed a couple of words. Already at this point I saw from his look that everything wasn't right. He seemed very uneasy. I had seen that look for so many times in my life that I knew what would happen, or at least I thought I knew. What happened next blew me away. I didn't expect that even though I had been in a situation like that before. But what I didn't expect was something so blatant I was about to experience. The CEO called a colleague nearby and said: *Can you handle this?* To me he said: *This person will take on from here with you*, and he went away. I stood there looking like a question mark until this colleague came to me and we moved to sit and talk around the table. This colleague was a decent guy and he asked me all the normal questions in a job interview.

At the end of the interview he however said to me: *I don't think we have a vacancy for you at the moment because we can get the IT students from the university to work when needed. But now we have your phone number and other contact information so if we have something, we'll be in contact.* That contact never materialized. What is noteworthy here, is that the unemployment agency didn't tell the company when they first contacted them that I was disabled. And why should they have? It doesn't have any effect on my skills and ability to perform in this kind of job.

The above mentioned situation is the most blatant example of putting me in an unequal position when applying for a job. It is certainly not the only one for I have had similar situations in the past, but they don't even come close to what I experienced this time. As sad as it is, I know I am not the first or the last that have had to experience that.

I would be willing to start working at this moment if there would be a job that would suit me regarding my limitations and if there would be someone willing to hire me. I would then be able to provide for myself just like any other tax payer. As long as this doesn't happen (disabled not being employed), the decision makers of this society should do something about the matter. Personally, it is very frustrating not being able to put into use the IT experience and skills I have gained during 21 years in a professional life. It is a pity that due to the prejudices in the labor market it cannot benefit from the effort of many disabled or people with limits."

PARENTS` THOUGHTS TODAY

Juha's family is very pleased that they chose the Kerland/Brainwave home- based treatment program at that time. It was a big deal for them. They are also content with how Juha is doing today and how he is able to live an independent life free from his parents.

Juha has developed a strong sense of resilience during the years. Thanks to this resilience he has achieved many things. The independization process started when Juha was 19 years old and when he moved to live independently close to his childhood home. He got his driver's license at the age of 21.

At the moment Juha's parents are worried of his employment prospects seeming impossible. The disabled and people with long-term illnesses are the unused resource in our society that is not being put into use in Finland. Some of these young adults are capable and have studied. They could work and provide for themselves if the society would change its attitude. Juha's mother is appalled by the treatment her son has received in the job interviews. How can people be treated like this in the 21st century, disabled or not?

Juha's mother says she has pondered a lot of times how Finland can afford to put all the disabled and young adults with long-term illnesses into early retirement? Wouldn't it be more economical to take into use their skills and develop an educational and employment path for these young adults where they would automatically move to when they reach a certain age? The mother thinks that these kinds of paths have been developed, but in reality they don't reach or offer possibilities to working life for many. She feels sorry for these young adults who would have capabilities to full day or half day work, but who have to settle for an early retirement. These young adults would also have the willingness to work and build their lives and fulfill their dreams. Each of them would want to be useful and do what their skills are useful for. Everybody should have the right to a feeling of being a worthy part of society and feel that their effort is needed.

Jutta

CHILDHOOD

Jutta is the third child of her family. Her first moments of life were dramatic. She was born overdue and she had lack of oxygen and her muscle tonus changed from limp to stiff. Both mother and child were *hanging from a thread* during birth. The doctor predicted that this child with cerebral palsy (dystonia tetraplegiga) would never walk. Jutta received the Finnish rehabilitation starting from three months old twice a week. Before she started the Kerland home-based treatment she could make crawling movements and crept in her own way and walked with assistance.

Age: 25 years

Home-based treatment started at the age of two

Home-based treatment lasted six years

Learned to walk at the age of eight

Wrote a poetry book at the age of 18, studies at the university

HOME-BASED TREATMENT

The parents heard about Kerland home-based treatment from a family they knew and after that they decided to go along with the program because they were ready to participate in more intensive rehabilitation than what Finland traditionally offered. The home-based treatment started when Jutta was two years old and it was first given four hours a day but later on the hours were reduced. Jutta participated in the program for a total of six years.

The home-based treatment time was very hectic in the family because organizing the daily program was the mother's responsibility. The family had their own company so the father's working days were long. He participated in the program when possible even though he was responsible for taking their two sons to sport practices and competitions.

It would have been impossible to execute the home-based treatment program without good assistants, say the parents. In addition to external assistants they had many relatives who wanted to help. It was also socially busy time because during patterning they talked a lot about what happened in the world. Most important was that Jutta's development was progressing. Also the positive feedback and support from the Kerland/Brainwave Centre staff felt good: *good girl, lovely, beautiful.* The parents thought that it was worth paying the money if only to hear someone praising Jutta and say what she can do.

Jutta's memories of the home-based treatment

"My exercise program was versatile. In the beginning there was a breathing exercise where I had to breathe into a special plastic bag. I remember it being one of the unpleasant exercises but it was left out of the program. There were also sit-up exercises for abdominal muscles which have developed my muscles so that I can now do 15 repetitions with ease.

My parents were committed to my home-based treatment and there was a lot of equipment at home for that. For example in one room there was a bar put into a bookshelf so that I could walk sideways holding it. My father built me a balance board where I developed my balance either by sitting or in a creeping position. For a walking exercise my father built a wooden channel where each foot had its own track. The idea of this walking channel was that I learnt to walk correctly by keeping my feet close to each other.

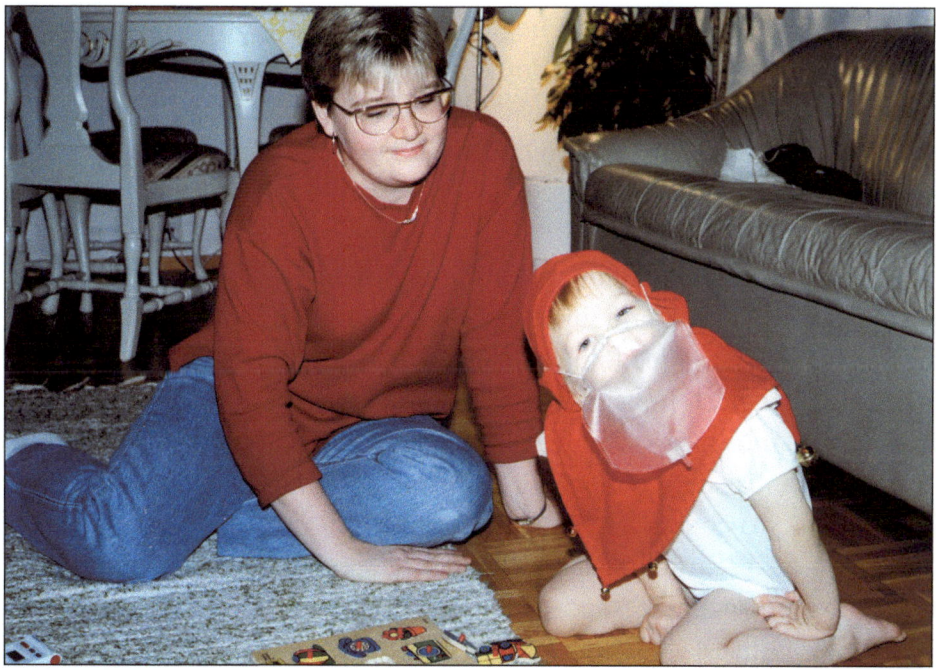

Breathing exercise.

I remember also an exercise which was called sprint movement where I was in a creeping position and I had to move opposite hand and leg forward and backward. I recall someone saying that athletes do that exercise also and for me it sounded very cool.

We had to travel to England to get me the program. I don't remember anything from that trip because I was so young. But I do remember going to the Kankaanpää rehabilitation Centre for the new exercise program. Those days were long because the adults talked about my rehabilitation and then we practiced the new exercise program. I recall one of the staff member in England greeting me in Finnish. I learned to introduce myself in English at the age of 4 or 5.

Surely I got bored at times in the Kankaanpää visits because the adults spoke only English. So I went to play on the floor. In the room where we practiced my exercise program there was a wooden slide and it was fun to go down the slide but climbing up was hard. I tried to climb the slide but of course I slid back down.

There were many people at our home helping out with my exercise program and I am so grateful to them. Each day we had assistants coming to our house because in the beginning sometimes three people were needed. In one exercise two people had to move my arms and legs and the third person moved my head. I don't remember the first meeting with the assistants but I remember that I liked them all. I still see some of those assistants because they have become my friends in other areas also.

A big help for my parents was also my three aunts who came to assist with my exercise program three nights a week. Also other relatives came to assist and it was nice to chat with them at the same time. In addition to the social aspect, their visits were important for I got a lot of support from them. And that is why I am so grateful to them all.

The home-based treatment program has been very beneficial for me. I have learned to control my body better and that has helped me learning to walk. I also learned social skills with all the new assistants. It also taught me perseverance and stamina which helped me to endure the control visits in the local hospital with all the different therapists and doctors during the same day and I didn't have to stay the night. I think that the home-based treatment also helped me to endure student life and other things in life also. Nowadays I can endure long days and don't give up too easily even though feeling tired.

If parents are thinking about their child's rehabilitation possibilities I would encourage them to put and effort into their child's rehabilitation even if the doctors were skeptical and say it is not worth the effort. If my parents had listened to the doctor back then and hadn't believed in my treatment I wouldn't be able to walk or function independently now. I am so grateful to my family for all the support I have received. Without their support and help I wouldn't be so independent today and without the Kerland home-based treatment I wouldn't be able to walk for a hundred or two hundred meters outside. And of course, I'm very grateful for the clinic staff, too."

SCHOOL YEARS

Jutta started school at the age of eight even though in Finland the normal starting age is seven. Jutta was small and she was born at the end of the year so it was reasonable to postpone her school start. Before that Jutta went to a preschool for two years. Before starting school Jutta's family contacted the principal so that Jutta's start in a normal school could be planned well ahead. Jutta was given an assistant whom she knew from her preschool. This made things easier for Jutta but also for the teacher because Jutta had the same assistant and teacher during four years.

The elementary school went well for Jutta. The only thing which annoyed her parents was that Jutta didn't have any good friend during that time. But she wasn't bullied at school which might have been because she always had an assistant with her. Before starting junior high school Jutta's teacher went to prepare the start into another school. Jutta's parents were grateful for this because moving to a normal junior high school wasn't so obvious for all the teachers; they were skeptic if this was the right place for Jutta at all.

These prejudices were due to the fact that there hadn't been a disabled child in that school before and that there was another adult present in the classroom. Moving to high school was fluent and Jutta was received without any doubts there because she had passed junior high.

During high school an assistant took Jutta to school in her own car because the school was in another city. After taking Jutta back home she helped her to take off her jacket and shoes and gave her a snack.

After the assistant left, Jutta stayed at home doing her homework independently. During summertime Jutta was at home alone because she didn't have an assistant then. Her mother prepared her breakfast and put some food on the table for snack. Jutta spent her day in front of a computer or watched TV or read books. Her mother came home from work around three pm and prepared dinner.

During the day Jutta's mother was worried of how Jutta was doing and hoped nothing bad would happen. Mother asked Jutta via SMS how she was doing. Jutta learned to be very independent and managed well at home alone especially during high school. The parents thought that Jutta had made a great impact on many people in her hometown and especially on teachers. Jutta has showed that anyone can manage when you have perseverance and resilience. It has been a lesson to learn for many, also for teachers.

Jutta also thinks that her school years went well. She knew already in the elementary school that she wanted to continue to high school and try to get into university. Jutta did well at school because she worked hard. Her plan was to finish high school in four years but she managed to do it in three

After high school Jutta spent a year at home because she went into a scoliosis surgery in the summer of 2010. It took the next winter to recover from the surgery during which she prepared herself for the big change, according to her own words. In spite of her disability Jutta has always wanted to live like any other of her peers. Jutta thinks that her dream of studying at university comes from the fact that it has been easy for her to learn different languages. As a child she dreamed of becoming a journalist so studying languages seemed like a natural choice.

A poetry book during high school

When Jutta was a child she wrote a lot of her own stories. At the age of ten she liked one book so much that she wrote a summary of it. The idea of writing the summary was to learn to write. In 2000 she wrote a poem to one of her friends and after that, writing stories changed into writing poems.

Jutta wrote the poems on a computer and made a collection of them. At first her poems told about nature mostly but after she joined an online group called Love poems she started to write about love and life in general. Writing to the Love poems page inspired Jutta because the other members could comment her poems. On the best days Jutta wrote three poems a day and during the years she wrote over 200 poems.

Jutta tells that as a child she dreamed of publishing a book when she was an adult. This dream came true when a friend of hers, Sirpa, found out that Jutta was writing poems. Sirpa read Jutta's poems and suggested that she did something with them. Sirpa organized an event where Jutta's poems were read aloud. The same fall they started to plan publishing a poetry book.

Going through the poems was a good thing because then Jutta realized that she had repeated some features in many of her poems. At times it was hard to listen to the feedback on her poems and how she should edit them. Some of the suggestions changed the poems so much that Jutta didn't recognize them as hers anymore.

Even though making the poetry book seemed interesting it was hard at times. Jutta was studying the second year at high school then and she had homework also. In the spring of 2009 Jutta had her matriculation examination so there was a lot to do. So she spent all the vacations of the year to edit her poems and planning the book. All in all, it was a learning experience to compile the poetry book.

After the book was finished the family organized a publishing event on Mother's day 2009 for friends and family. Jutta was handling the sale of her book mostly by herself and they were also on sale in the local bookstore. The demand for the book was great and the second edition was made and even the third during the spring of 2013.

Publishing the book was important and Jutta has received good feedback on her poems. She has been very pleased to know that her poems have touched the readers. Even though she has received support to continue writing unfortunately she hasn't done so. One reason for this is that Jutta needed to take a break from writing so that she can write a new kind of poems. The first poems were written by imagination but now she would like to write something about real life and thus influence the readers. Another reason for not having written more is that she has been busy with her studies and life in general. She hasn't completely given up writing poems but does so to her family and friends on their birthdays and other special occasions.

In addition to writing poems Jutta has also always loved to read because by reading stories she has been able to travel to other worlds. If the book is good and she has time, she can read almost for a whole day. She has been reading different genres but mostly love novels. She read all the Harry Potter books when they were published each. Lately she has been reading the work of Danielle Steel and Nicholas Sparks because they are light reading and they are dramatic. Jutta has also read stories based on true events like the books of Torey Hayden. Reading has been a good way to spend free time but it has also developed her linguistic skills. She has learned how to express herself by reading books.

If I Had Wings

If I had wings
I would fly on the sky
and see the world.

If I had wings
I would like to be as an angel,
who protects people.

If I had wings
I would go anywhere,
where I want.

If I had wings
I would hear voice of the sky,
which tells me a secret.

If I had wings
I would sleep on the clouds,
but how can do it,
when I don´t have wings.

LIFE TODAY

This 25-year-old student from Central Finland is quite happy and has a good sense of humor. She loves to write and especially poems. At the moment Jutta lives a very hectic student life in the city of Tampere where she studies the Finnish language at the university. Her goal is to get her Master's degree one day. So her dad's hope and promise of *I will make you a Master one day* might come true in the near future.

One of the greatest wishes that Jutta has is that her speech would become clearer and that her self-confidence would grow. She would like to live a full life like going to concerts, festivals and restaurants, see friends, travel and experience all the things that any normal person would do in their life. Also maintaining her capability to move is very important to her. Jutta wants to work as a writer in the future. At the moment she feels that her life is good because she has a nice apartment, her studies are going well and she has loved ones around her. Jutta says she wonders how well she has been able to manage an independent life during the last few years.

Jutta has been living in her own apartment in Tampere four years already. It has always been clear to her that she wants to move to live independently whenever it is possible and a suitable apartment is found. She didn't want to stay in her childhood neighborhood because there was no university or possibilities for different hobbies.

Even though Jutta's life has gone well she hasn't been able to avoid personal crises. Especially questions about womanhood have been on her mind. She has always dreamed of a family of her own. It seems that others have never thought that she should have a family, which makes her feel bad. She knows that pregnancy is a risk but if there are no obstacles in becoming pregnant she still dares to dream of it. She wants to do something meaningful in her life and raising a family would be just that.

Jutta tells that she has accepted herself and her limitations but cannot help making comparisons to her peers that don't have disabilities. Maybe forgetting her disability for a while and taking a chance have made her experience new things and to believe in her own capabilities. She has always wanted to do her best. When she was a child she thought that she didn't have her disability even though there were problems, and when she was about to move to a care home she felt uneasy. The thought of living with other people with disabilities made her realize her own disability.

Jutta's parents are happy about her success because she feels very comfortable in the city where she studies and she has a lot to do. Studying takes most of her time, of course. Her parents think that Jutta is very active and brave also even though her speech is unclear. Her bravery was notable last fall when she participated in the camp leader course and that gave her a lot of self-confidence. Jutta's parents think that she will get by in life with her gutsy nature and hopefully she will get an interesting job after her Master's

Student life in Tampere city

At first the move to the city of Tampere to study was scary to Jutta and also to her parents. But the everyday life of the parents got easier when the mother could work longer days and didn't have to worry so much of how Jutta was doing at home alone all day. A disabled child binds the parents tightly to the child's life and the worry doesn't end when the child moves away from home. At the moment Jutta lives 100 kilometers from her childhood home and her parents still worry about her.

Jutta was concerned of how she could trust strange people or how she would be understood because of her speech impairment. She decided to be strong because she understood that she needed to become independent at one point or another.

Jutta lives in a care home in the city of Tampere. It is a small building where each inhabitant lives in his or her own apartment and gets help from the staff when needed. In the summer of 2011 Jutta got to participate in a housing experiment and during that time her self-confidence grew stronger and the thought of living independently seemed right. Jutta said that she was very happy when she got the confirmation of her own apartment.

The move and adapting to live by herself went well. The city was familiar to Jutta and her other brother and some relatives lived there so it was easy to adapt. Of course it took some time to get used to cooking food, washing laundry with assistant and handling other chores. It also took time to get used to the conventions of the care home, for example during rush hour it might take over an hour to get assistance. So Jutta learned to ask for help well in advance so that she was able to leave on time.

Jutta believes that she will live in her current apartment for many years still. Even though she is happy with the care home the idea of an apartment of her own in a normal building tempts her. She would like to decide more over her schedule of when to shower and when to get help for cleaning. However, Jutta understands that a life like that wouldn't be so easy. She would have to look for her own assistants and take care of many things on her own. Jutta tried twice to enter the university but didn't pass the entrance exams so she started her studies in the Open University. She had lectures once a week which suited her life at that time. She was lucky to get her godmother to be her assistant with her studies and with grocery shopping.

Because studying literature went well and studying at the university seemed good for Jutta she participated in the entrance exam of literature and Finnish language for the third time.

She studied really hard during the last weeks and she thought that the exams went well but unfortunately she didn't pass either subject so the disappointment was great. Then she decided that she would make other plans for her future. However, the next week her big dream came true when her name appeared on the list of the accepted for the Finnish language. Her life got another meaning because now she had her goal to get her Master's degree.

Before starting at the university Jutta had to find a new assistant because her current assistant couldn't work a full day. So Jutta had to place a job advertisement on the internet and answer the applicants' e-mails. The number of applicants was a surprise because there were 20 people in all applying for the job. Jutta chose four people who visited her for an interview. She was supposed to choose one of them but at the last minute one of her friends told her that she knew a person who could be a perfect assistant for Jutta. It is important that the person is correct so Jutta met this person and decided at once to hire the person.

At the university Jutta was glad to realize how well the teachers and other students took her. After the first lecture Jutta decided to write to all the teachers about herself and mentioned the special arrangements she required like the extra time and the right to a separate space for exams. Since then it was much easier for Jutta to participate in the lectures because she had also explained in the message about her speech impairment that it was sometimes unclear but she could express herself clearly when given time to form sentences.

The other students took her well. Especially one tutor made Jutta glad when she promised to watch out with other tutors that Jutta could attend all happenings unobstructed. During fall Jutta participated in the freshman initiation party and in the Christmas party. She felt a sense of freedom when she got to let loose during the busy studying schedule because she had never experienced that. However, she didn't start to lead a wild student life even though she was invited to a lot of happenings. She preferred to stay at home. Because her study schedule had been intense in high school she decided to start the university at a bit slower pace.

Compared to the high school year she had to now reserve time for cleaning and other household chores. She also had to fit physio-, speech and riding therapies into her weekly schedule. She had only 10 lectures per week which was a good pace for her. The first exams went better than she expected so she felt she was studying the right subject. Even though she had passed the entrance exam she was still hesitant of how she would cope with studying at the university.

Bustling life

The fall of 2012 was an exciting time when studying at the university brought new content to Jutta's life. She got to know new people and made friends. Also her love life got a new turn when she met a man living in the same house. Mikko was the first person that Jutta could call her friend after she had moved to the building. Both of them come from the same place but they didn't know each other before even though Jutta had heard of and seen Mikko back home. Jutta got acquainted with Mikko in the activities of the care home.

She was scared to talk to him because her speech was unclear sometimes so they wrote Jutta says she had a crush on Mikko for some time but as a shy person she couldn't approach him. When Mikko told about his feelings it made her happy. They started seeing each other and make visits to each other`s homes a couple of times a week. Jutta had hoped for years that she would someday find a boyfriend just like her friends did. She had had crushes before but they weren't mutual. She had wondered if she would ever be good enough for somebody. So it took a while before she really believed that she now had a person in her life who wanted to be with her.

"It has been great to discover during these years that my feelings for Mikko have deepened. We agreed at the start of our relationship that we would save saying *I love you* for later. I am glad we agreed that because only now talking about love feels right. We try to see each other at least two nights a week, even though we live in the same building we have such busy schedules. Setting up a date outside our home has been difficult due to assistants.

I hope in the future we could be able to visit places together. Especially our two-year anniversary in 2014 was wonderful because we went to eat out in a restaurant and spent some time in the city after that. My biggest hope for the future is that our love will last. It would be also wonderful if we could make our dream of starting a family, come through. I couldn't wish for more."

Dancing and music

After moving to the city of Tampere Jutta also gained new hobbies. The first winter she started wheelchair dancing on the invitation of one of her neighbors. It has proven to be a good hobby because it strengthens the mid- section of her body. Listening to music has always been one of her hobbies so she gets to listen to music at the same time. She dances with an assistant as a combo so that the assistant is standing up. Even though it looks like the one standing is dragging the one in wheelchair, in reality the one in wheelchair uses her sides to turn the wheelchair. It took some time for Jutta to realize that she can turn with the help of her sides and not her arms. Jutta is now very happy that she has come a long way as a dancer.

The other benefits of wheelchair dancing are that you get to meet friends there too. In the spring of 2012 Jutta participated in a wheelchair dancing camp. Even though the weekend was tough the camp was really useful and exciting too because it was the first sports camp Jutta had participated in.

The first year of studying at the university didn't leave much time for wheelchair dancing due to a busy schedule. The next year Jutta didn't have a partner for the dancing and so she finally forgot about it and concentrated on her studies. In the third year at the university she began the wheelchair dancing again but had to quit again due to back pain.

At the moment Jutta hasn't completely given up dancing. In the fall of 2014 she got to experience a whole new side of wheelchair dancing when she made a choreography for her favorite song with her physiotherapist. For Jutta, planning and performing a dance choreography was the best moments of her life because she danced almost five minutes with her own body. This event was recorded on a film and Jutta acknowledges that watching the moment brought tears to her eyes. The dance began lying down followed by standing up on knees with hand movements with scarves.

The most exciting moment of the dance was when the dancers stood up on their feet and danced standing up moving from side to side and turning around. Even though the knees were bent and the dance was a long way from perfection, Jutta felt really good. She felt proud of herself for enduring a two-minute dance on her feet. After that dance Jutta started to trust her own abilities and she decided to start dancing on her feet without the wheelchair.

She still likes the wheelchair dancing but she wants to experience the joy of dancing with her own body. In the wheelchair dancing you use your stomach muscles but without the wheelchair you have to use your whole body. Jutta feels that this kind of dancing is very beneficial to her because she is sweating during the dance and her heart rate goes faster. She doesn't need a partner and she can develop choreographies for her favorite music.

Jutta has been a camp leader also and during the summer of 2012 she participated in an international equality camp where both disabled and normal children participated from different countries. This camp had a big difference to Jutta's self-esteem because she had to use the English language on the camp. When they were searching new camp leaders for the fall of 2014 Jutta decided to take the chance of a lifetime.

Happy camp leader

As a first-timer, organizing a camp was exciting for Jutta but it was also challenging due to her speech impairment. After living independently for four years Jutta's speech has cleared and she has gotten the courage to talk to strangers. Fortunately, the camp leaders were familiar from the camp the previous year so Jutta could trust that they interpreted and helped her. The organizing schedule of the camp was left to the last minute. It was a real concern that there wouldn't be enough participants on the camp but luckily they got 10 people to come along.

Organizing the camp brought a nice change into Jutta's fall because the camp leader crowd gathered to plan the camp and sometimes they came into Jutta's apartment also. Jutta told she was very happy after the camp that she had the courage to become a camp leader. The camp itself was an excellent experience and it contained excitement, fear, joy and pride. Jutta managed to talk in front of the whole camp also. When it was needed, other camp leaders interpreted her speech. One of the moments of success was when she got to help the campers with the words in a word scrabble.

In the beginning the camp leaders were a bit worried about the fact that two severely disabled children were participating in the camp. But this fear turned out to be useless for since the first evening the campers took the habit of helping each other out regardless of their disabilities, which was one of the principles of the camp. Jutta was happy about the fact that the campers were like one big family and could share their emotions freely, just like on the first camp she participated in. Being on the camp did good to Jutta because she saw how people managed to get by regardless of their many disabilities. She enjoyed more being the camp leader than just a camper.

When the camp was over, the campers sat in a hugging circle and cried over the end of the camp and having to say goodbye to new friends. Jutta says she will apply for a position of a camp leader in the coming years as well. She wants to do her part in making sure these kinds of camps continue because they are good for disabled people to experience camp life and the feeling of e quality.

Jutta's close relationship with her brothers

Jutta says she is lucky because she has two older brothers who have always supported her. The brothers have treated Jutta as if she didn't have any disability. Jutta thinks that her childhood would have been very different if she had had two sisters. They would probably have pampered her too much. From her brothers, she doesn't feel like she received any special treatment. Jutta feels that she learned to defend herself during sibling quarrels. Her brothers didn't come into rescue immediately when Jutta asked for help. Many times she had to ask more than once. But still, her brothers took care of her when she was little and their parents were not at home.

Now that all the siblings are grown up and live their own lives, her brothers are still very dear and important to Jutta. They all live in the same city and close to each other, so Jutta gets help from her brothers when needed. The brothers visit her every now and then and they watch TV together and talk about all matters of the world. Jutta will that their relationship would remain good and relaxed.

My dear Brothers

Could you protect me
from all injustice, evil.

Could you hold my hand.
Don't let me fall into the gap, gloom.

I know I will always be love for you,
nobody can ever change that.

You will always be in my life, forever.
My dear brothers.

Jutta's brothers have also good memories of their childhood. The years of the home-based treatment were demanding times for their whole family. Their father's sisters were assisting in the treatment but also Jutta's brothers had to help with the exercises. They didn't enjoy it much because they had other things to do also.

The brothers remember best when modeling and spinning were done to Jutta. And the mask for enhancing breathing was interesting to them and they wanted to test it too. The most memorable moment for the brothers has been when Jutta stood up independently for the first time. Since that moment she has been progressing in moving independently. The brothers think that the hours spent in rehabilitation have not gone into waste, but they have had a visible effect on Jutta's coordination and balance.

Afterwards the brothers have been wondering how committed their relatives were to Jutta's rehabilitation. The exercises required physical strength and movement from the assistants as well. They had to come from far distances after a working day to assist, which made it difficult.

The brothers think that Jutta didn't receive any special treatment in her childhood. They all are used to the little quarrels amongst siblings. The brothers are very proud of how well Jutta has done with her studies, and with success. They think that Jutta is the most gifted with language in the family and probably the most hardworking. The only thing separating Jutta from completely healthy people is that at first it might be hard to understand her speaking. But usually the second time things get clear. Jutta is also patient if you ask her to repeat what she said, she won't get frustrated.

During her time in the city of Tampere Jutta has become more independent like any other young adult, according to the brothers. Through her independence, Jutta has formed her own circle of friends which fills up the days of an already busy student life.

At the moment the brothers are living quite close to Jutta so it is easy to get together. Jutta is very important and dear sister to the brothers. Next, they have planned a pizza-night.

Louhi

CHILDHOOD

Louhi was born as a nine points girl, premature who had seizures. It was suspected that she was blind too. At her first moments of life her mother was told that she shouldn't expect anything from this child with cerebral palsy (tetraplegia spastica). At first the medical experts thought that rehabilitation wasn't worth trying because Louhi wasn't a reciprocal child. This opinion changed after one ophthalmologist's medical examination. So Louhi started to receive physiotherapy before she turned two years.

Age: 30 years

Home-based treatment started at the age of seven

Home-based treatment lasted two years

Learned to speak

Musical hobbies

HOME-BASED TREATMENT

At first the family had heard about the American Glenn Doman Institute at the end of the 1980's and later on they heard about the English Kerland/Brainwave Centre. The enthusiasm was great and so the family traveled to England in order to familiarize themselves with the method and to request an assessment of their child's situation.

The family starting home-based treatment caused a lot of conversation and doubt. *What witch doctor are they taking their daughter to?* it was whispered in the hospital. The parents were told bluntly that their decision wasn't reasonable. They had to defend their decision and they were warned about starting a foreign rehabilitation program. *How can you not understand that you can't do this when there are no scientific research results* was the advice from a leading neurologist to the father.

When the family got to know about the English home-based treatment program they realized how different its attitude towards children was compared to the Finnish healthcare system. The parents say that here in Finland it is emphasized what the child doesn't have, whereas in the Kerland/Brainwave program it is emphasized what the child can do. The point of view is not at all the same for the parents either.

The parents of disabled children frequently talked about how bad reputation they had with the healthcare personnel because they had the courage to question and set demands for their children. This was apparent especially when they told they would start home-based treatment program. It was quickly dismissed by the healthcare personnel without even a conversation based on proper knowledge. The parents thought that it would have been easier to give up and believe the Finnish medical experts.

Louhi's mother thinks that the parents of disabled children usually trusted blindly to what they were told and received depressed what they were given. Louhi's mother herself felt her own confidence rise gradually and she had the courage to defend her actions. The last resort she would use was *We`ll meet in court.*

When the home-based treatment program started Louhi was seven years old and it was continued for two years' time. The program was stopped for four months because the family lived abroad. Some parts of the program were done at school because Louhi was already going to school. The assistants took care of the exercises at school and at home, after school the rest of the daily program was done.

When the treatment started Louhi's upper body control was weak and she kind of hanged feebly. Thanks to the home-based treatment Louhi learned better control of her body and hands and also use of eyes. Her breathing got better also. However, she still sits on a wheelchair and needs assistance in almost everything. Nowadays Louhi can sit very well. She doesn't have any contraction nor has she needed any surgeries. The home-based treatment program contained a lot of motor skill exercises like stretching, breathing exercises and gymnastic exercises.

The most surprising development happened right after the start of the program. Until then she hadn't been able to speak even single words. After the start she learned to form words during two weeks` time at a rapidly growing pace and after two years she could speak – not fluently but pretty well. Nowadays she can communicate reciprocally and express her wishes and thoughts. Quite a leap for Louhi for the rest of her life!

One part of the treatment program was a mask exercise (a breathing bag) and showing word cards, which helped for their part her speech development. Louhi has always been positive and glad about the home-based treatment. Her family thinks that Louhi's development as such wouldn't have happened with Finnish rehabilitation methods only. Her home-based treatment program has been presented in magazines and two times in the national TV documentaries.

Louhi has received her daily doses of vitamin pills for years. Apparently she hasn't had much respiratory infections thanks to them. Louhi has a special diet where glucose and glutein are avoided. The home-based treatment program was beneficial for Louhi in terms of life control and quality. Her parents have been very pleased with it even though it was done at their own cost. And Louhi herself is feeling good about the results.

SCHOOL YEARS

Louhi's first school was a subject to debate. The psychologist thought that Louhi wasn't even apt for school. The parents disagreed and the psychologist said: *Don't you understand I have a six-year education for this. I know better than you.*

Fortunately, Louhi was accepted to school where there was an understanding principal and a teacher. They made an individual curriculum for Louhi where the home-based treatment program exercises were included. Louhi attended an education aimed at less disabled children. In the curriculum skills and readiness to survive independently in society are practised. These are, for example, communication skills and readiness for working life. Louhi also attended two other schools in the city of Jyväskylä. Going to school for Louhi was made possible by a couple of key persons' positive and valuable input.

LIFE TODAY

Louhi is a 30-year-old, severely disabled young woman, the only child in her family. She is interested in people and matters and she is also a very tenacious young woman with a good and lighthearted temper. She lives at home in south-western Finland. Her family doesn't plan to organize a carehome living for her. The assistants took care of the exercises at school and at home, the rest of the daily program was done at home.

At home Louhi has a full-time assistant to help her out and to do things with her. Louhi listens to audio books and music, she also likes to play instruments, sing and make all kinds of crafts. She receives music therapy once a week where she also practises reciprocal functions of her body and independent movement with a wheelchair. She also does wheelchair dancing and goes to the activity center's daily activities three times a week. During days Louhi still sits on a wheelchair. She receives physiotherapy twice a week and part of it happens in the swimming hall as pool therapy.

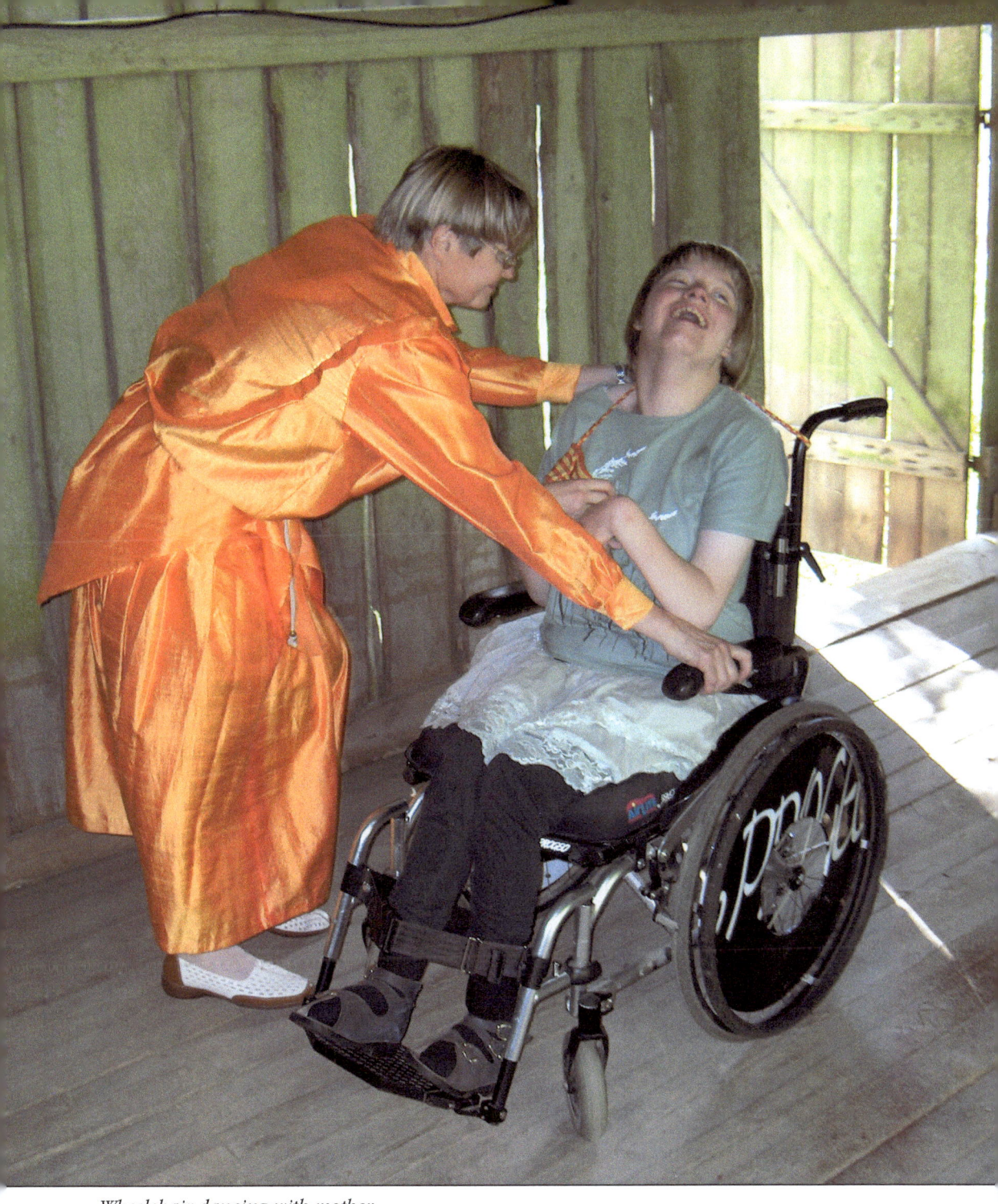

Wheelchair dancing with mother.

FATHER TELLS

I am a physician and retired Professor of Biochemistry at the Kuopio University. Besides teaching I have done research at cell and molecular levels and also on human subjects. I have worked at the pediatric departments of Helsinki University and Stanford University (USA).

We had two reasons to consider home-based rehabilitation for Louhi. First, it is a common knowledge that exceptional and skillful individuals often tell that they have behind them a long and intensive training program. Second, around that time there was an increasing accumulation of research reports on the plasticity of human brain and it was thought that it may explain development of various skills during training. So it was only natural to ask whether the home-based treatment program (15 hours a week for two years) could result in more positive results than the standard physiotherapy in our country (2 hours a week) or other types of therapy.

We learned from other families that a number of families had already visited the Kerland Centre in England. Mrs. Tarja Tallqvist (a journalist and later a member of the parliament) suggested that the interested families could found a society for home based therapy (RAMPPI), which was done soon after.

As chair of RAMPPI for almost ten years I received first hand knowledge on the Finnish families involved. I also visited the Brainwave/Kerland Centre several times and performed research with the Centre personnel on their records of children who had visited the Centre for treatment over years.

The Kerland/Brainwave Centre follows the principles of treatment developed by Glenn Doman in the United States. Many other similar programs have since been developed in Europe. They all have the same leading principle – plenty of repeated exercises for a long period of time. The treatment at home is necessary since the official treatment programs of the society are not interested in incorporating these elements in them. Many voluntary outside helpers (assistants) are usually needed in addition to the helpers available at home.

The neurological treatment of children is at a high level in our country. Among other things, treatment of epilepsy and for example, corrective surgical operations are well planned and organized. The society covers most costs of the necessary help devices. The home county helps in costs of living arrangements and transportation. In the U.S., for example, the family must cover these costs unless there is a suitable insurance taken. As a result, very few electric wheelchairs can be seen in the U.S. However, in neurological rehabilitation of children there is still much to do as has been the case also with adult patients.

Unfortunately, attitudes also make changes difficult. Parents of disabled children sometimes meet opinions which can be described as unprofessional, as many examples also in this book exemplify. Being a parent of a brain-damaged child is a heavy and long lasting task and the parents can remember well opinions expressed by the healthcare personnel.

Valuable exceptions to this exist. In our case, for example, we want to mention professor Lennart von Wendt, who was the leading child neurologist at the Lastenlinna hospital in Helsinki, and ophthalmologist Lea Hyvärinen, who is docent of developmental neuropsychology and professor h.c. of rehabilitation. Von Wendt had already in his early career in Sweden acquainted himself with home-based treatment programs and he had done research on these families. Hyvärinen is internationally a well known expert on vision research. She in fact found out that Louhi was responding to visual stimulation and Louhi´s rehabilitation was started as a result. In addition, docent Tuomas Westermark has stressed the importance of the quality of food and the need of vitamins and minerals for the neurological well-being of disabled children.

Home-based treatment programs have been criticized because the results have not been scientifically documented. However, scientific reports can be found by using internet search programs. Some neurologists have based their critical opinions on the fact that there is no *textbook knowledge* on the programs. However, there are a number of books published on these methods. Case reports are often based on single patients. The reason is that there are many difficulties in arranging treatment experiments with large groups, since the children are of different age and their disabilities differ. And how to arrange a control group? In addition, research is costly and there are again difficulties in getting funding and in publishing the results.

Knowledge on the structures of brain and their basic functions are now very well documented. However, the detailed functioning of the brain is still largely unknown. Therefore, one must have on open mind as to the efficiency of new types of rehabilitation programs. Recent results on the plasticity of the brain help to understand the results of rehabilitation. Nevertheless, it is difficult to understand why, for example, the speech development of Louhi was very quickly initiated during the treatment program. My own guess is that the mask breathing caused an increase of blood and possibly brain pH. Mr. Kai Kaila, professor of neurosciences at Helsinki University has recently described experimental results on the joint regulation of nerve cell pH and GABA receptor functions. In any case, Louhi must be satisfied with the development of her speech skills and the new ways to express her wishes.

Knowledge on the prevention of cerebral palsy would be more valuable than the long-term costly and demanding rehabilitation. On visiting the Brainwave Centre, we discovered that many CP-children were born during weekends. We did calculations on this finding and found out that statistically this was true. The control group consisted of children born with Caesarean section and children who had a chromosomal abnormality. However, these findings proved to be difficult to publish in scientific journals. However, one leading neonatologist in Finland commented that *it is easy to believe*. Fortunately, in recent times deliveries are increasingly taking place in larger hospitals with various kinds of medical experts at hand. This is definitely better for children.

The results of home-based treatment programs can be regarded as modest in relation to the degree of disabilities. However, even the results can be of great importance to the quality of life and future options of the children. Lets think for example the development of speech skills of Louhi, the developed walking ability of Veikko, who was able to just crawl as a child, and the ice hockey goals Jani demonstrated. In this connection the comment of the TV-journalist in the "Ajankohtainen kakkonen" (Current two) program was well thought: *In a small country among the small circle of specialists there are sometimes strange arguments on matters, for example, the importance of treatment programs. Jani if anybody can say that only the goals count. The result is the most important thing.*

Memme

CHILDHOOD

Memme is a girl with cerebral palsy (tetraplegiga spastica) who was born two months too early. She got a severe (third degree) cerebral hemorrhage right after she was born. Before she was transferred to another hospital she was given an emergency baptism. A nurse sprinkled water from a small porcelain cup over the head of Memme in the incubator.

Age: 27 years

Home-based treatment started at the age of six

Home-based treatment lasted three years

Learned to stand, vision, speaking and social skills got better

Horseback riding as a hobby

Memme has received Finnish physiotherapy a couple of times a week since she was six months old. The purpose of physiotherapy was to break the strong tonus in her body. She learned to move on the floor rolling.

One of the most important things in Memme's life has been horseback riding and a pony called Duffis which she got when she was three years old. When the family heard about riding therapy they got very excited and the next thing they did was to buy a pony. The family knew a girl who had a pregnant mare in the stables they went to and that mare had a foal in 1993. They went to take care of the pony on weekends. The stable was really cozy with its smells and animals and it became the weekly visiting place for Memme's family where they could enjoy country life and eat and drink on the hay bale.

Many of the girls on the stable got to train Duffis before a disabled child like Memme could ride it. After four years of training and growing up, Memme got to ride her own pony. A shoemaker made a special vaulting belt for Memme to help her with riding. Her parents walked by the pony and one of the stable girls lead the pony.

When another girl was born into the family the hobby with horses continued with her. Duffis the pony reached the age of 20 but the last years he suffered from illnesses. Finally, the pony had to be put down and the family made the very hard decision in the spring of 2013.

Ponygirl riding Duffis the pony.

HOME-BASED TREATMENT

The family read about the alternative rehabilitation methods from magazines and they also visited one Centre in Finland where they learnt more about the matter. They got very enthusiastic about the Kerland/Brainwave method which was started when Memme was six years old. During three years Memme received home-based treatment and went to school at the same time from a long distance and that is why the home-based treatment could only be given after the school day. The daily dose of treatment lasted only two hours, sometimes even less. Later on riding therapy was started which became a long time hobby.

The below presented program is very versatile and compact where there are exercises for visual areas, balance, joint movement and muscle stretching and strengthening.

1. Visual Training (1min)
2. Hip Unlocking (1min)
3. Heel Cord Strech (1min)
4. Push against Wall (1min)
5. Pelvic Lifts (1min)
6. Trunkal Pattern (1min)
7. Cross Pattern (2min)
8. Command Crawl (2min)
9. Table Strech on back (1min)
10. Table Strech on stomack (1min)
11. Pole exercise (1min)
12. Adductor Strech (1min)
13. Vestibular Board crosswise (1min)
14. Vestibular Board lengthwise (1min)
15. Shoulder Loosening (1min)
16. Push ups (1min)
17. Quad Position (1min)
18. Hip Unlocking (1min)
19. Heel Cord Strech (1min)
20. Push against Wall (1min)
21. Passive Cycling (1min)
22. Cross Pattern (2min)
23. Ladder (3min)
24. Stand at bar (1min)
25. Free stand (1min)

During the program Memme learned to crawl and to stand up. In addition, her body tonus, head control and eyesight got better. Moving around for Memme is difficult due to two surgeries on her hips after which she has started getting epilepsy seizures. But her social skills and also speaking and conversation skills have developed during the home based treatment program.

SCHOOL YEARS

Memme went to a school in Jyväskylä for 12 years with a distance of one hour one way in a taxi. The school was meant for children with disabilities in functioning or learning or for children with neurological damages school or a long-term illness. Both Memme and her family thought that the school was excellent in many ways especially for its premises and staff. Cooperation was seamless and the most important was that there was joy of learning in everything and the children supported each other. Memme had many friends in the school.

Her parents thought that Memme was a popular student because she was social and outgoing. In the school Memme has learned to recognize letters and sounds and can write with a computer from a model. She hasn't learned to read yet but she is really trying.

LIFE TODAY

Memme is a 27-year-old happy and social young woman from Central Finland. She is learning to be independent. She goes to a preparatory school which is a good place to learn independence and readiness to a life of her own. Acting in a peer group is very important in the development of a young person's self-esteem. During the weeks Memme lives in the school and for weekends she comes home. In the beginning Memme was against moving to another location: *I don't want to move anywhere from home.* Little by little she has gotten used to living away from home.

Her parents wish that in the future Memme could live independently in a care home. This wish is actually coming true in the near future. Memme has expressed conditions for moving to a care home: she needs an assistant and during summer she wants to go to the market to buy peas.

For Memme the best subjects at school are music, home economics, English and IT. On the other hand, she doesn't like physical education or mathematics because she isn't allowed to use a calculator.

Memme needs help with everyday tasks. She can walk when assisted and she has a new lifting device to help her out, but her mom was against it at first. That is why Memme calls her mom with a nick name. Memme receives physiotherapy twice a week and she also goes to horseback riding once a week. Also swimming and girl scouts and listening to music from computer are her hobbies.

In the future Memme wants to continue horseback riding which has been the family hobby for 22 years. Looking back, the most important memories from the stables are the smells. Her mother thinks that it has been important for Memme to get used to big animals and to new people.

Also traveling is an important part of Memme's life and that is what she wants to do in the future also. She has visited Turkey four times, ten times in Greece and once in USA.

Memme´s parents think that hobbies are very important in a child's life because then they can maintain a balance between work and free time. Horseback riding and traveling have offered Memme a lot of new experiences. Especially during summertime going to the stables and spending time in the nature has been an important part of the family life. Her parents think that all the young people like Memme should have the possibility to study to a profession and to work if able to. That would give them self-confidence and raise their dignity.

Salla

CHILDHOOD

Salla is the firstborn of her family and she has a brother, five years younger than her. Salla was born two weeks overdue. During birth she suffered from a severe lack of oxygen and she had to struggle for her life. But she was a tough girl and she survived. The diagnosis doctors gave her changed many times in the beginning. Finally, she was diagnosed with cerebral palsy (dystonia tetraplegiga) and she

Age: 24 years

Home-based treatment started at the age of five

Home-based treatment lasted two years

Learned to walk at the age of eight

Recently graduated to a youth and leisure instructor

received Finnish rehabilitation starting from when she was a baby due to her difficult birth and because she had unusual muscle tension changes in her body. First started physiotherapy and speech therapy at the age of two, then riding and occupational therapy at the age of five. Salla received these therapies 3 – 4 hours a week but her parents thought it was not enough. Before starting the home-based treatment Salla could crawl and creep in her own way and she could also walk holding a support.

HOME-BASED TREATMENT

Starting the home-based treatment Salla's parents found by coincidence a book by Linda Scotson called *Doran: Child of courage* (1985) from their local library. After reading the book they wanted to know more about that kind of rehabilitation method. Her parents thought that Salla's good response to rehabilitation and her cognitive skills were evidence that she had a lot of so-called healthy reserve in her brain which had to be taken into use by rehabilitation. Earlier it was believed that new nerve cells are not formed to replace damaged ones but in this new rehabilitation method it is thought otherwise. Nowadays the brain research has proven that the plasticity of the brain is much greater than thought before.

When Salla was five years old she started the tight Kerland/Brainwave home-based treatment program which lasted two years. At first the family had to travel to England but later on the Centre in Kankaanpää, Finland. Salla received rehabilitation about 15 hours a week, sometimes even more. The program for Salla concentrated on moving her limbs alternately and learning to use her hands more precisely. At the same time her muscles strengthened which made learning to walk possible. Salla learned to walk at the age of eight, in spite of the doubts of the doctors.

The parents thought that it was important to make the home-based treatment for the child by adding songs, stories and play into them. Salla herself thinks that the biggest challenge in the rehabilitation of a child is how the adults get the child motivated into doing the exercises. There is a big difference in trying to get a child to do a boring exercise compared with telling an adult that when you do this you get certain benefits from it.

Salla remembers all the different methods the adults used to motivate her to do the exercises: toys, stories and playing. Exercising outdoors with her family was important to Salla because it was a good daily form of exercise. There are a lot of uneven surfaces and stimulation for the senses in the yard outdoors.

Salla's own description of the first visit to the Kerland Centre

"When I was five years old I went with my mom and my godmother to Bridgewater, England. Of course we had to try this method. Which mother wouldn't do her utmost for the wellbeing of her child? So one fall evening we went by plane to England. My father stayed at home with my six months old brother. It was my first trip abroad and of course I was excited about what would happen. The travel went well and we arrived in London where we first took a bus to Reading train station. By train we went to Taunton where the clinic's physiotherapist Phil met us and took us to Bridgewater. On the train I remember wondering a big horse-shaped area which was seen far away on the hill. I was so excited about a train-travel that I licked the window and probably got stomach flu from it.

Fortunately, that stomach flu passed quite quickly. At Bridgewater Phil took us first to an apartment next to the Kerland Centre where we would stay the nights. We had our own kitchen, bedroom, toilet and shower. After settling in we went to the Centre where I got to explore the playroom first. From the Kerland Centre I remember the playroom, toys, colors and the staff. My rehabilitators were Phil, Carl, Heidi and another woman whose name I don't recall. I remember being shy when they asked my mom and my godmother and me to the rehabilitation room for the first time. And that was the only time I was shy there. I had a toy cat at that time and I pulled it from a string after me. This cat was to protect me when we first entered the rehabilitation room. When Phil noticed my cat he said aloud in clear Finnish language kissa (cat). So Phil had my confidence.

A moment later I was lifted to the exercise table. *Relax* said Phil when they started to do the exercises to me. I remember lying on the table when the adults moved my arms and legs. This is how it was done: right leg and left arm were moved up, and left leg and right arm were moved down, and vice versa. This movement is called patterning which means that my brain got a correct picture of creeping and walking.

I was also placed to walk on *a hand ladder* that is a kind of wooden ladder placed horizontally on top of four wooden pillars. So I was underneath the ladder and moved my hands from one bar to another and walked. I was like Tarzan moving from one liana to another. I also remember the bouncing, motorized ball which motivated me to crawl on an exercise mat. Crawling has never been my favorite past time. I liked the bouncing ball so much that they let me have it and take it

After the days at the Centre we returned to London. The train station where we arrived was Paddington station. My mom said smilingly that I resembled Paddington Bear with my small suitcase. That made me smile too because we had read the Paddington Bear's adventures just before traveling to England.

In London, after a long day of traveling, I wanted to go out for dinner. My mom and my godmother were tired but we headed to the nearest hamburger restaurant. I think I was more interested in the English people there than the hamburgers. The next day we moved around London and visited a huge play store where I could choose toys for myself and for my brother. We headed back to Finland after two days in London."

Exercises and their effects

The home-based treatment was started directly after the visit to England. An exercise table was purchased and the hand ladder. The municipality gave an assistant during weekdays to help out Mom with the program. Mother was on maternity leave at the time and father was working normally.

The exercises lasted two hours in the morning and then there was a break. During afternoons there was another two-hour set. The program contained for example patterning, walking on uneven surface, walking with the hand ladder, crawling and creeping. Salla remembers that she didn't quite like crawling so sometimes the whole family crawled to motivate her. In addition to the Kerland program Salla received Finnish rehabilitation two hours a week. The home-based treatment program was stopped when she went to school.

Now as an adult Salla has pondered over what she thinks of the home-based treatment she received. She thinks that the program has been beneficial to her. Despite all the painful examinations in the hospital the home-based treatment has gone well. She learned to walk independently at the age of eight which was due to the Kerland/ Brainwave method. Also positive feedback from parents, grandparents, other relatives, friends and the people who assisted in her program, has motivated her. The people she has met have been most important for her. Salla says she many times thinks that how many people she wouldn't have met without the home-based treatment or the disability. It can only be guessed.

Her parents see the effects of the program on especially on Salla's social skills. Doing the exercises were social events. Due to the program the contacts and stimuli for the child grew in number. Also the amount of positive feedback was sure to increase her self-esteem. The strong self-esteem and good social skills are necessary for any young person trying to grow more independent. Salla's parents think that the principal goal of program was to strengthen and learn physical skills. In addition, the child received important mental assets from the adults.

The home-based treatment started to show the strengthening of the muscles, the development of certain fine motoric skills and learning to walk independently. The parents think that program can be compared to practising athletics: regular and sufficient practice with time to rest is essential for achieving results.

Salla's parents wish that Finland's official health care would give the parents a clear rehabilitation program adjusted to each child's needs. The rehabilitation cannot rely just on professional therapists but needs to engage also the child's parents and other close members of the family and friends. Therapists and other rehabilitation professionals should work as coaches and supporters of the family.

For Salla's family, the decision to take part in a home-based treatment program wasn't a protest against the therapists working with them. The work they did was and still is very good in quality. The quantity just wasn't enough. The home-based treatment brought more needed quality and quantity into the family's own participation in the rehabilitation.

Afterwards Salla's mother has gone through with the therapist whether the home-based treatment had an impact because there is no-one to compare to. Would the development have progressed anyhow? The therapists answered: *I am convinced that there has been a great impact; so many other similar cases have gone through my hands.*

SCHOOL YEARS

Salla was the first disabled child integrated into a normal school in her town. At first, the most resistance came from the teacher but she decided to face the challenge and made incredible work for the success of the integration. The worst option for the mother would have been a local school for special need children, which was far away in another town. So the decision was to integrate Salla into a normal classroom, especially when the results of the school readiness tests with perception testing done by the central hospital encouraged to this. There were no cognitive hinders to start in a normal classroom. The biggest challenges might have been in the attitudes and lack of practice.

Some of the parents wanted that Salla would be in their kids' class. Afterwards Salla's parents have received good comments about her school attendance. The family agrees that the choise was best for the child. In the mean time her peers got acquainted with disability and hopefully most of the prejudices vanished.

Nowadays there is a special school merged as a part of a normal school in Salla's home town. The children with special needs study as much as possible integrated into a normal classroom of their age group. The ninth and tenth classes Salla attended in a special school in the city of Kuopio. It was a relief for her to get a break from her special status and to get a peer support at that age.

At high school Salla says she worked hard but got tired during the last year. She didn't graduate because she didn't pass the English exam. Foreign languages were difficult for her.

LIFE TODAY

Salla is a 24-year-old student from Central Finland. She is social by nature, thoughtful, empathetic and she has a good self-esteem. She has just qualified as a youth and leisure instructor. She studied two years far away from her home. Her mother's relatives lived nearby so she had a safe environment around her.

After the studies she is planning on moving into a bigger city in the North of Finland where there are better chances in the work life, studying and versatile hobbies. And also her friends live there.

Her hobbies are drawing and painting which she has done since the school years. Her dream is to learn to play the harmonica so that she can get her lungs exercise at the same time. Salla writes a blog and connects with people on facebook. Salla received in December 2015 a new sportier model of a wheelchair and she has started to exercise 1-2 kilometers daily in the nearby sports field.

Her studies

Salla started her studies in the August of 2013 and they lasted two years. Salla was lucky to pass the quite demanding entrance exams well. She was the only person with cerebral palsy in the course. She lived in a dormitory in connection with the school where there was a special room for disabled with bigger bathroom than the other rooms. The kitchen was shared with other students in the dormitory. The campus was designed so that there was an unobstructed passage everywhere so it was easy for Salla to move around.

Salla got an electric wheelchair so she could move longer distances independently. She could also walk independently but it was wobbly. Her speech was clear enough for a stranger to understand also if they had the patience to wait and listen.

In the daily routines she required physical help especially with transfers from one place to another. Salla needed two assistants for her daily routines which came to help her from Tuesday to Thursday in two shifts. On Mondays and Fridays she had only one assistant due to lesser need for assistance for traveling. Salla traveled by bus each Friday to her uncle's house in a small village where she spent her weekends and returned to her dormitory on Monday mornings. Traveling by bus was possible with the help of an assistant to get her into the bus and paying to the chauffer. At the destination there was always another person to receive her to help her out of the bus.

In her studies the subject of the classes changed weekly. It was a custom that one subject was studied during one week. Usually there was an exam at the end of the week where the knowledge of each student was tested. Sometimes there was no exam but the subject was graded against a so called *continued evidence* or a learning diary. One time they had a project regarding the use of intoxicating substances and the object of the project was to inform facts about intoxicating substances and what happens when consumed. The students gave lectures about alcohol, internet behavior, tobacco and snuff.

Presentation to other students

Salla wanted to give a presentation at the beginning of her studies regarding her disability. She wanted to inform the other students of cerebral palsy and how it affects her life. She gave the facts and also personal experiences of her life.

Salla first clarified the term cerebral palsy and to which things the disability affects and how it is caused most likely. She also went through the definitions of cerebral palsy and developmental disability and explained that these two are different disabilities even though some severe cases of cerebral palsy also have developmental disability also. At this point Salla had noticed a change in the audience's minds and that she had changed the attitude of the audience towards people with cerebral palsy and hopefully also towards people with other disabilities.

After defining the term of cerebral palsy Salla told about herself and what caused her to have that disability and the starting point in her life, the diagnosis she got and what kind of childhood she has had. She also clarified what kind of rehabilitation opportunities and aiding tools there are and what needs to be considered when acting with a person

As a lecturer in Haparanda, Sweden.

with cerebral palsy. At the end of her presentation she showed a video clip of a young boy with cerebral palsy. The video explains in detail the life of a child with cerebral palsy, the aiding tools and especially about the joy of life. After the presentation the audience had a chance to ask questions. Salla received a positive feedback and the audience thought that the presentation was very enlightening and emotional. Salla herself says she was in a bit of a shock to notice people crying in the audience. Her assistant cries every time she hears Salla giving a presentation.

After this presentation the attitude in Salla's school changed and she was considered as an equal student and a friend. The presentation was so good, according to the teachers that Salla has given about ten similar presentations already to other student groups and she even traveled to Sweden to give a presentation in an international seminar in the fall of 2014. Salla's teacher, who has asked Salla to give presentations to her special pedagogics class, says that Salla will not become a youth and leisure instructor but a lecturer. Who knows what the future brings.

Facing the prejudices

When Salla started her studies she encountered prejudices at the school. Being different was scary to many people. Salla tells she noticed her class mates also having prejudices against her and so many of them tried to avoid her. Salla's unclear speech, wobbly walk and dyskinesia caused doubt in people and also having an assistant and using a wheelchair or the electric wheelchair were uncommon in the small town.

Each person with cerebral palsy has faced prejudices in their lives. Salla herself remembers the first time she understood the prejudice against her was at the age of ten. She thinks there were those before also, but she just doesn't remember. Salla thinks that a child's mind is clever in surpassing these memories and considering them as normal.

The most common prejudices she has faced have been long looks on the street, in public places like grocery stores and even in the hospitals from the health care professionals. The best way to recognize a prejudiced person is when they speak to a disabled person like to a child or to pass them in a conversation like they didn't exist but address only the assistant. For Salla this kind of behavior is disturbing if an adult speaks to her assistant instead of directly to her. Salla says she usually answers the questions herself. She doesn't want to just nod and try to please others. The biggest prejudice that a person with cerebral palsy comes across is that people think that all disabled are also mentally disabled. Salla thinks that this is due to lack of education in the schools.

THE YEARS OF GROWTH FOR THE PARENTS

The endurance of the parents is at stake when a disabled child comes into the family. There start the years of growth for the parents towards a demanding parenthood. The mother of Salla describes this as a life-long school with not much evaluation of how well you have done. Typical of this schooling is that the studies are binding and demanding. It is as hard as for other parents, multiplied by a hundred. You have to reconsider your own values and attitudes very deeply. This comes across when the running of each day sucks the marrow out of bones in the endurance of the parents.

Salla's mother says that you get to participate in children's play with a physically disabled child in the family reunions and parties. One parent gets to talk with other adults in calm at the coffee table when the other has to act as an assistant to their child. In addition to the basic care, the parents have to act as their child's secretary in the different public offices regarding their child. Your communication skills get better and you become good negotiator who doesn't bow or lose their nerves. Here also you are on a continuous learning curve when situations and needs change.

The parents have to learn to anticipate because they always have to be a little bit ahead of things and try to anticipate needs and wishes. Little by little the parent becomes an excellent planner and organizer. If the mother works also, she gets to rest there and has other things on her mind and adult company. Burn-out is always sitting on your shoulder as a parent of a disabled child. Your own feeling of insufficiency and guilt, horror pictures regarding the future and feeling of hopelessness crush you like a hurricane when you don't have the strength anymore.

Salla's mother tells that she wouldn't have survived alone but needed another person to reflect her feelings and emotions. Their family was lucky to get an excellent therapist who pushed them through the hard times and listened to the despair without falling under the pressure herself and who had the talent of asking the right questions.

After years of hard work Salla's mother tells she is very happy to have gone through that phase in her life. It has shed away the unnecessary need to achieve and grown honesty towards oneself and to other people. Salla's parents hope that they have been able to give wings strong enough and roots deep enough to Salla, so that she can fly on her own and when crashing down, be able to get up again on her wings.

Sanni

CHILDHOOD

Sanni's first moments in life were spent in the ICU. She was put into a respirator in the ICU right after the birth by the requirement of her mother. Sanni was born with the help of an epidural as a nine points girl eight weeks too early. Her mother thinks that Sanni appeared to be full-time with long hair and brownish skin. At the age of just one day Sanni got a minor cerebral hemorrhage and started having seizures.

Age: 25 years

Home-based treatment started at the age of one

Home-based treatment lasted six years

Learned to read and write at the age of five

Developed material with her speech therapist to the Pathway –communication folder

When Sanni was six months old her parents started to worry about her development. She had problems with controlling her head, for example, so the parents wanted better medical examination and they got it. However, the doctors tried to calm them down by saying there was nothing to worry about, but that didn't reassure the parents. Thus they took their child to a private doctor in the city of Helsinki and that doctor sent Sanni to another medical examination to Lastenlinna children's hospital and there it was discovered gradually why her motoric skills weren't developing normally.

HOME-BASED TREATMENT

Sanni's parents got interested in the foreign rehabilitation methods when they read the book by Linda Scotson *Doran: Child of courage* (1985). In that book the parents actively rehabilitated their child. The mother of Sanni was eager and ready to do more for her child because she was at home at that moment. The mother also studied so when the father came home from work, the mother went to study. Sanni's home-based treatment started very early. She received treatment by both Kerland and Delacato methods partly at the same time.

At first they got to know the Kerland program which started when Sanni was one-year old and after a year parts of the Delacato program were introduced. The mother compiled a suitable combination. The home-based treatment was done during six years during which magazines were interested in writing about the new kinds of rehabilitation methods.

The mother guessed that they were one of the first families in Finland that participated in the Kerland program. The fact, that they made a designed program for each child at the clinic based on the child's strengths and that the child was treated individually with the disability being part of the child were appealing aspects for the parents. The parents thought that in Finland the child's disability was too much the center of attention.

Sanni's family sought after an assistant for the treatment by putting notes on the walls of grocery stores. They got 5 – 10 people working in the treatment circle and their good friends helped out also. Later on they got a child minder and a health care student to assist at home and they executed the program during daytime.

During the home-based treatment Sanni's head and body control as well as physical condition got better. Her muscles started to develop different from before. Sanni has gone through two hip surgeries, the first one at the age of five. They were prepared for a long period of recovery but Sanni's good physical condition made her recovery faster.

Sanni's daily program included physical exercises and also looking at pictures and words, also combined, and word cards. She learned different concepts quickly and this might have influenced her learning to read and write at the age of five. At preschool Sanni had already good language and sound recognition skills which helped her in learning to read. At the age of twelve she wrote to a Mother's Day card: *Mother, you are brave when you set things in order.*

The exercise program below is one example of Sanni's daily program where there are many breathing, balancing and modeling exercises and also joint movement and standing exercises.

1. Mask (1min)
2. Pictures
3. Hip Unlocking (1min)
4. Trunkal Pattern (2min)
5. Roll Pattern (1min)
6. Stand (1min)
7. Mask (1min)
8. Swing: arms and legs (1min)
          arms (1min)
          legs (1min)
          arms and legs (1min)
9. Sit (1min)
10. Mask (1min)
11. Hip Unlocking (1min)
12. Trunkal Pattern (2min)
13. Roll Pattern (1min)
14. Stand (1min)
15. Mask (1min)
16. Reciprocal Pattern (5min)
17. Mask (1min)
18. Assisted Crawl (3min)
19. Ramp (2min)

Like many other Finnish families, Sanni's family faced a lot of resistance against this foreign rehabilitation method. Sanni's family had several experiences from different hospital and rehabilitation periods from Finland. The attitudes of the healthcare staff were visible especially in the beginning when the family told they were participating in a foreign home-based treatment program. *Hopefully you understand as parents that you might not do the best for your child with this kind of behavior. Just be parents.*

SCHOOL YEARS

Sanni went to school according to a normal curriculum until the tenth grade. The days were long. At seven a.m. she was picked up by a taxi to school and she returned home at five p.m. During school time Sanni had time for horseback riding, swimming and wheelchair dancing. At fourth grade Sanni wrote her own poem for the school magazine: "UP in the tree, nearby the school, George the Squirrel is sitting. A smile was dancing on the lips of the mother-Ninni while acorns where falling down on George the Squirrel. Luck was shining on George the Squirrel while acorns were pouring down."

When Sanni moved to secondary education she created contents with her speech therapist Marja Liikanen to a communication folder (Pathway – communication book with partner assisted auditory scanning) which was published by The Finnish Association on Intellectual and Developmental Disabilities.

The Pathway folder is based on partner assisted auditory scanning. It is meant for such users who cannot point out pictures or words but the different choices are read aloud to them by auditory scanning. The model doesn't emphasize word order by Finnish grammar but the focus is on starting with the main point which is then complemented into a sentence form.

The Pathway folder can be used for three different messages: 1. if there is little time, only the readymade messages are done, 2. the creative messages according to the scanning pathway, 3. free messages are built according to situational clues where the adult is describing different options or clues for the particular situation. The fact is first searched among the pathway and then the free scanning is used for completion.

Sanni has also gone to a specialized college which she finalized in the spring of 2013. After that she has planned independently her weekly program along with the daily activities.

LIFE TODAY

Sanni is 25-years-old and the second child of her family, she has an older brother. She has cerebral palsy (dystonia tetraplegiga) and she requires full-time personal assistance with all daily activities, also with communication because she doesn't speak but uses the auditory scanning folder or writes. Sanni likes to cook so that she guides the assistant in cooking. At her heart Sanni is a food lover, but it doesn't show on the outside. Her favorite activities are listening to music and different audio books.

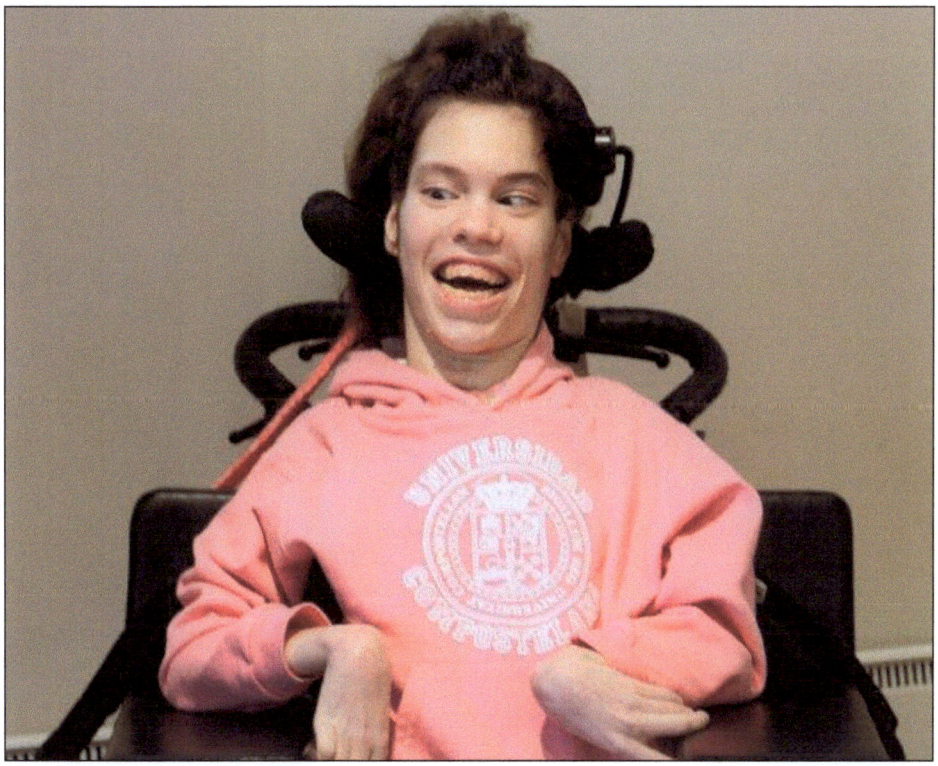

The favorite thing to do for Sanni is listening to music and audiobooks.

Together with her personal assistant Sanni goes to the activity center three times a week. The group consists of other young people with physical disabilities, the same age as her. On other weekdays she plans her daily program along with the therapies. Her favorite activities are also shopping, going to restaurants and cafes, and swimming. She also likes traveling especially to different cities. Sanni has had the opportunity to visit most of the European countries and she is at the moment saving money for yet another trip.

Sanni still receives physiotherapy twice a week. She can move by stepping when assisted. Her future plans include moving to her own apartment. Friends are important to Sanni so she wishes she can move to a communal housing.

Tiia

CHILDHOOD

Tiia is the youngest of five in her family and was born seven weeks premature. After birth she suffered from cerebral hemorrhage which, according to her parents, appeared during blood transfusion. Her parents were very concerned about Tiia's eyesight because she still didn't respond with her eyes at the age of five months and didn't smile at anything else but lamp light. On the other hand, her hearing was excellent which disturbed her falling asleep in the evening.

Age: 26 years

Home-based treatment started at the age of one year and four months

Home-based treatment lasted four years and six months

Learned to speak at the age of three, vision enhanced

Sings as a hobby

At six months´ age Tiia started to have spasms and she was given an ACTH medication. After starting the medication Tiia should have regained her eyesight. But since after a couple of months nothing happened the doctors suspected that she was blind and would stay that way. Tiia received physiotherapy since she was 10 months old three hours a week.

HOME-BASED TREATMENT

Tiia's family found out about the home-based treatment from a family they knew and who were practicing the program at that time. Before that they had read everything about rehabilitation. The parents thought that they could also try out the home-based treatment program their friends were practicing. So they started to do the exercises from the Kerland program independently. One of them was flashing a flashlight in a dark room for activating the areas of eyesight in the brains. Surprisingly enough during three months of practicing the exercise Tiia started to show development. She, for example, started to reach for objects using her eyesight. Tiia's mother still remembers the first moment because it was Christmas Eve. Her mother was feeding Tiia and while Tiia was eating her mother put a toy in front of her eyes and suddenly Tiia grabbed it with both hands.

The family participated in the official Kerland program for four and a half years. The tight scheduled home-based treatment started when Tiia was one year and four months old. In addition to the traditional movement exercises the program included eyesight stimulation like watching pictures and words. During the program Tiia's eyesight developed little by little. Tiia also learned to crawl and creep correctly and take steps with help. When Tiia finally learned to creep, one of the assistants burst into tears of joy.

The program gave a very tangible operating model to be and do things with Tiia. It also stimulated mentally. Modeling and its intensive social aspect significantly affected Tiia`s learning to talk at the age of three. The program also gave Tiia's elder siblings a model how to act with and talk to Tiia even though she couldn't actively seek other children's company.

The home-based treatment had a big influence on Tiia but also on her mother's self-confidence. *For me as a mother it was very important to be able to do something for my child especially when the traditional Finnish rehabilitation didn't produce enough results from our point of view. As a mother I think that Tiia wouldn't have a mentally healthy mother if I hadn't been allowed to do something for my child. My mind required*

Tiia coming down the ramp.

action. Later on the child could blame the parents for not having done anything earlier. Tiia's parents were scared that she could blame them when older for not having done their all in regards to her rehabilitation. They felt that time was running out and soon it would be too late to rehabilitate.

The family recruited the assistants by delivering 300 letters in the neighborhood. They told in the letter what kind of assistance was needed and that it was completely based on volunteer work. This way they were able to organize an active circle of assistants of 35 persons. Some of them assisted throughout the whole time of Tiia's treatment and some only for a little while. And some of them became lifelong friends.

The trainers and doctors didn't see the home-based treatment with approval. They thought that it was based on too passive repetition and it was contradictory to the Bobath method used in Finland. The skeptics also thought that the other children of the family didn't receive enough attention suffering from the rehabilitation of Tiia. But Tiia's own physiotherapist approved the Kerland method and supported the parents. Years later this same physiotherapist praised Tiia's parents and said that, if this family hadn't done so much for Tiia, she wouldn't have been able to move in an upright position.

The other children of the family have been glad afterwards that they also got to travel abroad when they went to the Kerland Centre in England. *We have been fortunate to have a possibility to travel abroad. Without the trip to England we wouldn't have been able to travel.* On the other hand, when the home-based treatment program was practised, the bigger children didn't like all the assistants coming in and out their home. *Again with the assistants.* One of the children stood before the exercise table with intention to block the way. This kind of resistance and jealousy was seen at first.

The parents saw, however, that the tight home-based treatment was more constructive than destructive for the family. Today the siblings are on very good terms and they all love Tiia very much. An evidence of this is the fact that all the children of the family came home from all over Finland to celebrate Tiia's 22nd birthday.

SCHOOL YEARS

Starting school was a difficult time according to Tiia's parents. Tiia's parents or doctors didn't know what would be the best form of schooling for Tiia. The mother tells that they pondered a lot about learning difficulties and what caused them; is it epilepsy, visual impairment or cerebral palsy and to which degree Tiia is disabled. For a couple of years Tiia went to a school meant for physically disabled but from there she was finally moved to a classroom for autistic children even though Tiia was a very social child.

Most of her school years Tiia went to a primary school for children with disabilities where she was the only physically impaired during many years. During the last years Tiia many times refused to go to school but she liked the afternoons in the daycare. In the daycare there were many children without any disabilities and they made contact with Tiia and so she felt more comfortable there. The mother says that learning to read in a normal classroom would have been more supportive than in a classroom for autistic children. One reason for not having learned to read might be the visual impairment.

When the family visited an ophthalmologist at the Finnish Federation of the Visually Impaired the doctor showed Tiia figures meant for illiterate people: a house, an apple, a flower etc. Tiia didn't answer anything. Then the doctor changed the cards into four times bigger and then Tiia started to answer. She just hadn't seen the smaller cards.

LIFE TODAY

Tiia is a 26-year-old young woman who lives in the Päijät-Häme region in a care home. She has her own room and she really likes living there. Almost all the residents are young people with disabilities. Three times a week Tiia goes to daytime activities in the Kaarisilta art and activity center. In the care home she is encouraged to move around independently and her helped walking has gotten better. Recently Tiia has been accepted into the vocational studies for music, which is a three-year education.

Before the care home Tiia lived in several different temporary care homes but she didn't feel comfortable in those and missed home all the time. She got to know her current care home at the age of 20. The group living in the house was just about to be formed and the boys talked Tiia into it.

Tiia got very interested in the new place and her parents thought that it was a real answer to their prayers that Tiia was happy with this new place.

The next door neighbor of Tiia is a nice young man and together they sing. Tiia has a really pretty singing voice and she has a good pitch so she learns new songs easily by heart. She also sings in the parish choir and she goes to church every Sunday. There she has friends that help her moving around and dressing and take her to coffee after church.

By nature, Tiia is a happy and social person and usually content with her life. She talks a lot and that's why her next door neighbor calls her a weird chatter. Tiia's long time hobbies are drawing, painting and horseback riding. She has also learned how to use a camera. Before Christmas, Tiia started making pearl bracelets for her family and friends.

She still has a severe visual impairment but she can function in familiar places relying on her eyesight. However, she has developed a lot and sometimes her family and friends forget that she has the visual impairment. She can see little details, work with her hands and Tiia receives physiotherapy 2-3 times a week. She can reel a wheel chair and take steps with help.

Physiotherapy is extremely necessary to her because without it Tiia will regress and her feet start to hurt. Even the smallest break can cause problems. Also horseback riding has proven to be very important to Tiia's physical condition. There is a horse close to the care home where Tiia lives and she gets to ride it every week.

Artwork by Tiia.

Unsku

CHILDHOOD

Unsku is a nick name for Juha. He was born as full-term nine points boy. At the age of one month he suffered from whooping cough which is very dangerous for a small child. The mother suspected that her child got the cough from one of the surrounding families because they didn't want to vaccinate their children. Since birth Unsku has had weak lungs and thus problems in breathing.

Age: 24 years

Home-based treatment started at the age of three

Home-based treatment lasted six years

Learned to stand leaning against a support, joints and muscles got stronger

Listens to music

He spent most of his first year in the hospital due to examinations done to him. His diagnosis was developmental delay.

He started receiving physiotherapy at the age of three months two times a week. He received a diagnosis for the Angelman syndrome at the age of six. Unsku is a typical Angelman child (angel child) with weak lungs and scoliosis and in addition to developmental disability he has weak speech development and epilepsy. With Angelman children the developmental delay is noticed usually before they turn one-year old. Delays in physical movement, eating problems, minor need for sleep and slower growth development than normally are typical first symptoms.

Angelman children are happy and easily get enthusiastic, sometimes they are hyperactive. These children learn to walk clearly later than their peers, usually at the age of 3 or 4. Their movements are not precise. Other characteristics for these children are epileptic seizures, repeating laugh attacks and twitching hands and tapping. Angelman children hardly can speak at all and that is why teaching sign language and picture communication is very important. Luckily there are many instruments and methods for communication available.

HOME-BASED TREATMENT

The mother had heard only good things about the Kerland home-based treatment. Two families they know were already practising it so the mother of Unsku had the courage to take part. When Unsku was not yet three years old they traveled to England with a family they know to start the home-based treatment program.

Unsku received the home–based treatment three hours daily for six years' time. And even after they stopped the program they still practiced some of the exercises. One part of the home-based treatment was a mask exercise which helped getting breathing better. There were also color and shape learning with cards, which Unsku learned. The program was a big factor in maintaining Unsku's joints and muscles in good shape during the home-based treatment. He was able to push himself up from a sitting position but he has never moved independently.

Unsku's mother thinks that the two scoliosis surgeries he went through diminished the chances to move and if he hadn't been doing the home-based treatment program his joints would be all stiff in a hooked position and the situation would be much worse.

The mother was solely responsible for Unsku's treatment but she received help with doing the program. Once a week there were ten different assistants helping out at home. From the unemployment agency they received two itinerant workers. This circle of assistants worked really well. In addition, they received help from relatives. For example, one relative constructed a ramp for Unsku to practice crawling. The ramp resembles a slide so you get to feel the forward movement. All the

Breathing exercise with belts.

assistants put their best effort into the program and they didn't doubt its effectiveness.

One of the neurologists treating Unsku had seen on TV a program regarding the Kerland/Brainwave home-based treatment and he didn't consider it bad if the family had the strength to practise it. When Unsku's mom said to one Finnish neurologist that the family is willing to receive Finnish rehabilitation, the neurologist answered: *Leena, you have the right attitude.* So the mom suggested to the neurologist that: *Why don't you organize a similar circle of assistants as in the Kerland home-based treatment. Plan a program with the therapists and give instructions and correct minutes for each exercise for us parents and we will execute it. If you just tell us that we could perhaps try these exercises at home, nobody bothers to do them.*

SCHOOL YEARS

Unsku's experiences from school have been positive according to his mother. The first years he attended the special curriculum, which was designed for children with severe disabilities. In this curriculum the subjects have been integrated quite tightly with treatment interaction. The curriculum is divided into four categories: motor skills, communication, social skills and daily skills. These categories replace the normal subjects in the elementary school.

When Unsku's diagnosis was confirmed the then head of the local education and culture department suggested that Unsku should be moved to a normal class room with a personal assistant. Those years at school were the best, according to the mother, and it was good for the normal children to get accustomed to a disabled child. Unsku's mother thought that he received so much of everything. In addition to learning he was accepted with love into the class room and he was taken along to all activities. He was the center of attention in the class in a positive way. And when Unsku had his birthday the whole class came to his house to celebrate.

LIFE TODAY

Unsku is the youngest of the family. In the summer of 2014 he moved to a care home close to his family. Before the move Unsku practised living in the care home every now and then during two years. After the first not so easy days Unsku is now very happy in the care home. His mother visits him a couple of times a week to spend time with him outside among other things. Unsku goes to an activity Centre or the severely disabled from the care home four times a week. There he has many kinds of activities like music, movies, physiotherapy and sensory practices.

Before moving to the care home Unsku lived together with his mother in their house. He needs assistance in all daily activities and he sits in a wheel chair during the day. His mother had to get up two to four times a night to roll him over to another side. During the last few years taking care of Unsku alone had become too heavy for the mother due to the fact that she had to handle everything alone and the sleep debt was starting to take its toll.

Unsku's father was away traveling around the world for his work so it was time to think about Unsku's future. On the other hand, it was a scary thought for the mother not having Unsku around because she was so used to taking care of him. Unsku's mother thinks that she has also done a huge favour for the society, because the town has been able to save hundreds of thousands of euros while she has been the career of her son during the 23 years.

All in all, Unsku is a very happy young man who cannot speak but he understands when spoken to. He has a good memory and he sees and hears very well. He has his own ways of expressing himself, like when he feels hunger or thirst he snaps with his mouth and with his eyes he can show what he wants.

Unsku's favorite hobby is listening to music, which brings him a lot of joy and laughter. When Unsku was living at home they sometimes used to go swimming, theaters or concerts with his mother. Also shopping and watching Finnish soap operas were his favorite activities. Unsku did exercises every day so that he stood up with the help of a standing frame and after that he pedaled on an exercise bicycle. At home he had good equipment for exercising and he used them meticulously.

Veikko

CHILDHOOD

Veikko was born as a nine points boy. During birth he suffered from lack of oxygen and for that reason he was put into an incubator for a week. He is categorized as severely handicapped because he has a developmental delay due to chromosome abnormality. At the age of one it was noticed that his development wasn't progressing normally and a chromosome test was taken. The abnormality (46XY11Q+) was so rare that there wasn't any explanation for it. He received physiotherapy starting at the age of one. In the beginning the family was told that the chances of Veikko learning to walk were minimal and so the family shouldn't expect anything because these kinds of children don't learn. But Veikko surprised everybody.

Age: 27 years

Home-based treatment started at the age of three

Home-based treatment lasted three years

Learned to walk at the age of five

Plays drums

HOME-BASED TREATMENT

The family received information of the Kerland Centre from women's magazines. However, the parents contemplated long and hard before starting the program, whether it was worth taking the risk and trust your child's natural development or to start working on it. They came to the conclusion that they didn't just want to sit and wait but started the tight scheduled home-based treatment, and they haven't regretted it.

The family had very skilled assistants, some of them were hired and some neighborhood friends. Many times the children of the assistants joined in playing at the same time as their mothers were helping out in Veikko's rehabilitation. The mother of Veikko remembers those times as having fun together. The other children in Veikko's family seemed very natural with all the treatment activities. As the father of the family was earning the living, the mother was mainly responsible for the home-based treatment. The life at that time was also hard and busy according to the parents, but that was their life.

Veikko was almost three years old when they started the intense home-based treatment program which continued for three years. Before they started the program Veikko could move around by sitting on the floor with the help of his hands or crawling in his own way.

Progress was seen after a while when the program was started. Veikko's whole posture got better and it seemed that he progressed all the time. The program schedule was tight and the mask exercise wasn't his favorite part. Veikko started to crawl and at the age of five he learned to walk independently. The family of Veikko didn't face any criticism from the Finnish health care staff towards the Kerland/ Brainwave program even though so many other families did. They were lucky to have an excellent physiotherapist working with them who participated fully. She traveled with the family to the Kerland Centre in England.

Veikko has undergone a few big surgeries. Almost right after the home-based treatment started he went into a heart surgery at the age of four. His hips and ankles have also been operated.

The home-based treatment program of Veikko has been an interest to many people and Veikko has been the model child for rehabilitation in his home town. The family has been showcasing the program all around the country. There are also small studies and theses made of Veikko.

SCHOOL YEARS

Veikko started school integrated into a normal class room with his assistant. This raised a few questions in other people: *Shouldn't these kinds of children be treated in some special school for them. Or –What kind of people do they accept here.* A special education teacher came weekly to guide the assistant and to work with Veikko. Going to school has always been pleasant to Veikko. Especially the school mates were important and he still looks at pictures of them eagerly after so many years. Later on Veikko was moved to a special needs school at the Honkalampi Centre, into which he went for four years. After that Veikko started at the Luovi vocational college in Käsämä which prepares you for an independent life and gives rehabilitating teaching and guidance.

LIFE TODAY

Veikko is a 27-year-old third child of his family and he still lives with his parents in eastern Finland. He needs a lot of assistance with everyday tasks and he has an assistant coming to help him at home three times a week. This assistance is stated in the law for the services for disabled, although not everything is offered from the municipality but you need to insist. At home Veikko likes to watch pictures from a tablet or a computer.

A couple of times in a month Veikko goes practicing living independently in a service home Menninkäinen which is maintained by the The Finnish Association on Intellectual and Developmental Disabilities. A proper housing model is being searched for Veikko. He cannot live completely independently but a community housing would be suitable. His parents think that Veikko is very adaptable.

Veikko doing his favorite thing.

Veikko cannot speak but he has his own ways of expressing himself. He has developed his own sign language. If he wants to be alone for example so he waves with his hand, or as a sign of acceptance he taps his fingers. Veikko has a good memory and sense of direction as well as a good sense of hearing and social skills. Veikko is living the moment. Veikko receives physiotherapy twice a week. Earlier he also received riding and music therapies. Veikko likes to produce sounds and objects that make noise like pot lids are his favorites. Especially he loves to play drums, which he started at the age of ten. Before that Veikko played the tambourine and the bongo drums. Because his enthusiasm for drumming was so great, his parents got him a drum set at home which is in heavy use.

Many times he asks one of his friends to join him playing the drums and that way gives a lot of joy to his family. Playing drums is very useful practice because it requires the use of two hands and even one foot to play the base drum. Playing loud is also a good way to release anger.

On the prevention of cerebral palsy

Pekka Mäenpää, Pirjo Halonen and Phil Edge
University of Kuopio, Finland (presently University of Eastern Finland)
and the Brainwave Centre, Ltd, Bridgwater, England

Summary

This study was initiated when it was found that many CP-children who arrived to the Kerland/Brainwave Centre for rehabilitation were born during weekends. Data of all brain-injured children who had visited the Kerland Foundation Rehabilitation Centre (presently the Brainwave Centre) between the years 1982 and1994 were analyzed. 254 children (172 born naturally and 82 by Caesarean section) were included. A control group with a history of essentially normal birth consisted of 79 children with chromosomal (29 with Down syndrome) or metabolic abnormality. It was found that the number of births during different weekdays were distributed unevenly (p=0.019) (chi-square goodness of fit test). The children with cerebral palsy born naturally were concentrated at or near the weekends with the highest numbers occurring on Fridays, Saturdays and Sundays. The lowest numbers occurred on Wednesdays and Thursdays (p<0.0001). The CP-children born by Caesarean section or children suffering from a chromosomal or metabolic abnormality showed no such concentration of births at or near the weekends.

The background of brain injury resulting in cerebral palsy is usually thought to be developments before of or soon after birth. This study shows that birth itself seems to be an important factor influencing development of brain injury in some children, since it demonstrated a dramatic concentration of births at or near the weekends among children with cerebral palsy born naturally but not among similar children born by Caesarean section nor among children with chromosomal or metabolic abnormality. It could be estimated that, for children born naturally, up to 47% of cerebral palsy may have been preventable, if the figures for the lowest occurrence in the middle of the week represent the best possible medical care. Further, the fact that the number of children born by Caesarean section did not show an increase at or near the weekends suggest that, among other approaches arranging the delivery units in larger and better staffed hospitals and increased use of Caesarean section in the connection of difficult births may offer possibilities for increased prevention.

Finally, since data on births and medical diagnoses are systematically collected in most countries more extensive studies on the basis of these preliminary results will be possible during selected time periods.

Summary of the becoming adult stories of the young

The stories of the young in this book showcase well the willpower, perseverance and hope of their parents. The same perseverance is present also in these young. Some of them are studying, all of them have some kind of a hobby and some of them have boy/girlfriend with whom they can plan the future.

It comes through from the life stories that these young live similar kind of life than their peers do, with their limitations. Most of them want to live independently. Some of them have already moved to live in their own home far away from their family or they live independently in a care home. Some still live at home with their family and participate in the daily activities for disabled.

One of the young adults is studying at the university and her goal is to get her Master's degree in the near future. One of her biggest accomplishments has been publishing her own poetry book during high school years. It is probable that her skills in writing will continue flourishing in the coming years. Another young adult has just gotten one degree and will continue studying for another. The third has gained an extensive experience in IT, but hasn't been able to get a suitable job. The fourth is just starting a three-year vocational education in music.

All of the young adults also have long-lasting hobbies where they can express themselves and at the same time bring joy to people around them. One writes poems, second paints and draws, third sings in a choir, fourth rides horses, fifth plays drums, and so on. Listening to music is the common interest to almost all of them. In addition, wheelchair dancing is the favorite hobby of two of the young women. Some of them use social media: twitter, facebook, instagram and blogging.

These young adults are often described as happy and social personalities. However, all of them still have different kinds of problems; one of them has difficulties in speech production and the other in walking. All of them require an assistant to one degree or another. All in all, these young adults have come a long way during the years which is best known by those closest to them.

In many ways these young adults and their parents have been pioneers. When starting school, almost every parent has had to discuss hard on which school is the best for their child. Most of the children were integrated into a normal classroom, at least in the beginning. They all had a personal assistant, which wasn't self–evident at that time. It is evident that the presence of an assistant has affected so that these children were not bullied at school that much.

The school years went well for most of the children, even though a disabled child in a normal classroom might have caused a lot of prejudices at first. In the society the prejudices and attitude against disabled are hard. The tight home-based treatment was usually ceased when the child started school.

Three of the young adults in this book have attended high school. One of them has graduated from high school and two haven't. The reasons for not graduating have been due to not passing some of the exams, like the English language or mathematics, or not passing some of the courses.

These families have also been the attention of media interest at that time. There are magazine articles and TV programs made of some of the families.

The future of these young adults causes a lot of worry because it is difficult to find a job for those who are able to work. The only option is early retirement which is not the best option for any of these young adults.

Willpower of the parents

The starting point for most of the children was difficult and it would have been very natural for the parents to believe some of the Finnish health care experts' often negative comments about the possibilities of development of their child. One can only wonder where these parents got their strength and trust in the future when they started the heavy home-based treatment program despite the negative comments from the surroundings.

When interviewing the parents, they expressed their disappointment at the amount of Finnish rehabilitation and towards the attitudes of health care experts and to the fact that they as parents weren't allowed to participate more actively in the rehabilitation of their child. It is important that the parents are encouraged and supported in their attempts to support their child's development, as it was done in the foreign centers. Just hearing someone say something good about their child and not just state the defects, brought a lot of joy to the parents. It is noteworthy, that none of the parents regretted the amount of work they were able to do for their child. The parents were happy with their choices even though the home-based treatment was hard and required a lot of resources during many years.

One reason for the families to be happy was that the home-based treatment started to show results after quite a short time since the program was started. The first development steps might have been small for an outsider, but significant for the family life. For example, if the child had by then woken up many times a night and after the everyday program started to sleep full nights, it was a great relief to the family. It was also good to have the child eating properly. All the families were happy to see their child's physical appearance and stamina getting better. The muscles started to develop better compared to before. This was apparent in the control of head and body as well as in better posture. Blood circulation also got better in the face and limbs. All of these factors made the everyday life easier and the quality of life better.

The most prominent development steps were noticed in motoric skills, like creeping and crawling movements and better use of hands. Many of the children learned to walk in one way or another, which isn't self-evident for a child with cerebral palsy. The father of one of the children, Jutta, evaluated the effects of the home based treatment like this: *I don't think that Jutta would walk and be so independent. I also don't believe that Jutta would be in such a good condition she is now without Kerland. Jutta is tenacious and resilient. Still, her walking isn't as perfect as with healthy children.*

Most of the families also mentioned that their child's social skills and ability to make contact got better during the home based treatment. These children have received a lot of attention because of the many people helping to carry out the program. The children have been discussed with, asked questions and pondered about things with. The children have been praised and encouraged. All this has had significance for the speech and thought development of the child as well as for building a strong self-confidence.

Thoughts after writing the book

I have been interested in the rehabilitation of disabled children since the 1980's as a helper and enabler. I have visited the Glenn Doman Institute in the United States, the Kerland/Brainwave Centre in England and the Delacato Centre in Belgium. I acted as the translator for two families with a child with cerebral palsy when they visited England and I have done my part in getting Doman to visit Finland and getting the Kerland/Brainwave Centre to establish a Centre in Finland.

Working at the university and giving lectures to people working with disabled children has given me opportunities to tell them about these home- based treatment methods. Especially the lessons learned from the Doman Institute and the books written by Glenn Doman have fascinated me in many ways. I took an interest in strengthening exercises of the visual areas where complete words written in big fonts (word cards) are shown to children. In the best cases, this exercise leads to learning to read before school teaching. This has happened to many children, also to disabled ones. This method of learning to read turned out to be such an interesting topic that I wrote later my Ph.D. dissertation about it.

When I became familiar with the rehabilitation of disabled children, I learned to understand the development of healthy children better. Supporting the motoric skills of children has been one of the central topics in my teaching work. I have learned to understand how important it is to children to learn to perform the basic movements (for example creeping and crawling) as well as possible. This means that children are able to creep and crawl reciprocally in a coordinated manner with their arms and legs. This is why in the program the children are first shown to creep and crawl with passive, assisted movement called patterning in order to get the feeling of them. Especially in the Doman and Kerland/ Brainwave methods, strengthening the motoric basis is seen a very important and all the other higher functions are built on that. In addition, stimulating the senses is important.

The home-based treatment programs have raised a lot of questions due to the method how they are carried out and the part parents play in them. *Just be parents* –type of comments hurt many of the parents. *Mother's love and kids TV shows are enough for a disabled child*, commented a leading child neurologist at that time. This person has probably changed his opinion during the years. The most common questions have been: Can parents rehabilitate their own child, shouldn't they just be parents? Would the results have been similar if these children had received the same amount of the NDT therapy used in Finland? Why are there so many passive, assisted movements in the program? Does the home-based treatment method suit all types of families?

Tight and long-lasting home-based treatment, based on the activity of the parents, doesn't necessarily suit all types of families. It might be a question of money, but more likely it is a question of family resources and motivation. The families in this book received a lot of help from outside but some covered all the costs themselves. Some home towns organized garden sales or relatives supported the family visits to England. The assistants were mainly volunteers and the family had to work on finding them.

The criticism by the Finnish physiotherapists was aimed at some of the passive movements, like patterning. Three adults are needed to carry out this exercise and it looks quite passive from the child's part. With this exercise the child's brain is given an idea of what creeping and crawling feel like. Gradually, when the child's ability to function progresses, the exercises are made more active on the child's part. The goal is to help the child reach a level of independency as high as possible.

The Kerland/Brainwave home-based treatment method is versatile. It isn't necessary to take the child from one therapist to another, but the program contains several types of therapies. There is a lot of communication with the child also. The vocabulary of the child is enhanced and the imagination gets richer with the assistance of different people. The changing assistants have the patience to talk and make questions of all sorts to the child. The child becomes more social easily. After the intensive home-based treatment program was finished, the amount of rehabilitation decreased and the families moved to more traditional practices.

It would be recommendable that the families of disabled children should have the possibility to attend such rehabilitation program as is best for their family. There should be no lack of assistants with the unemployment rate being so high in Finland and a lot of people are interested in doing voluntary work. This work is meaningful. It is noteworthy, that the best benefits for the child are received when the rehabilitation is carried out in cooperation with the experts and parents.

Thank you Juha, Jutta, Louhi, Memme, Salla, Sanni, Tiia, Unsku and Veikko and your parents for letting me write your stories into a book. You were real fighters and the first children who received the home-based treatment in Finland. Thus I want to appreciate the work you have done. This book is also an homage to the Kerland/Brainwave Centre. I thank my daughter Marianna Karvonen who proofread my texts and translated the book into English. I would also like to thank those of my friends who helped me in finalizing this book.

Summer's child

I wish I was a summer's child,
born in midsummer's beauty.

I would run across the fields of hay,
I would taste the fruits of summer.

I would dance through the nights,
I would swim all the time.

I would pick flowers,
I would give them to my love.

But I will cease to dream -
for I am not a summer's child.
Still, I will enjoy
each summer
as if I was a true summer's child

About the writer

Mrs Pirkko Karvonen has a Ph.D. in Early Childhood Education and a Master`s Degree in Physical Education. She has done her dissertation on teaching children to read before school age and specialized in physical education of children. She is called *the Mother of baby swimming* because she initiated baby swimming in Finland in 1981 from which she has been awarded with a golden decoration. She has also written children`s programs for TV.

Pirkko Karvonen has worked most of her career at the University of Jyväskylä in the Department of Early Childhood Education as a teacher and a researcher. She has published several text books of early childhood education. Juhan askeleet – kotikuntoutusta Kerland-klinikan menetelmällä (1999), the book about a boy with cerebral palsy who was rehabilitated with the Kerland method, was written inspired by the visits to the Doman Institute, Kerland/Brainwave Centre and to Delacato Centre.

Related bibliography

Karvonen, P. 1999. Juhan askeleet – Kotikuntoutusta Kerland-klinikan menetelmällä¬. Jyväskylä: Atena Kustannus Oy.

Delacato, C. H. 1974. The ultimate stranger, The autistic child. Novato: Academic Therapy Publications.

Doman, G. 1979. How to teach your baby to read. Philadelphia: The Better Baby Press.

Doman, G. 1984. What to do about your brain-injured child. New York: Doubleday & Company, Inc.

Doman, G., Doman, D. & Hagy, B. 1988. How to teach your baby to be physically superb birth to age six. Philadelphia: The Better Baby Press.

Le Winn, E. 1969. Human neurological organization. Springfield, IL: Charles C. Thomas.

Scotson, L. 1985. DORAN child of courage. London: Collins Publishers.

Selänpää, J. 2009. Keneen lie tullut. Mänttä-Vilppula: M-print Oy.